Macramè
FOR BEGINNERS

EMILY RIBBONS

© **Copyright 2021 by Emily Ribbons—All rights reserved.**

The content contained within this book may not be reproduced, duplicated, or transmitted without direct written permission from the author or the publisher. Under no circumstances will any blame or legal responsibility be held against the publisher or author, for any damages, reparation, or monetary loss due to the information contained within this book. Either directly or indirectly.

Legal notice:

This book is copyright protected. This book is only for personal use. You cannot amend, distribute, sell, use, quote, or paraphrase any part, or the content within this book, without the consent of the author or publisher.

Disclaimer notice:

Please note the information contained within this document is for educational and entertainment purposes only. All effort has been executed to present accurate, up-to-date, and reliable, complete information. No warranties of any kind are declared or implied. Readers acknowledge that the author is not engaging in the rendering of legal, financial, medical, or professional advice. The content within this book has been derived from various sources. Please consult a licensed professional before attempting any techniques outlined in this book. By reading this document, the reader agrees that under no circumstances is the author responsible for any losses, direct or indirect, which are incurred as a result of the use of the information contained within this document, including, but not limited to, errors, omissions, or inaccuracies.

Table of Contents

INTRODUCTION — **8**

CHAPTER 1. WHAT IS MACRAMÉ? — **11**

Some Items to Gift to Your Friends

CHAPTER 2. BASIC MACRAMÉ KNOTS — **16**

Square Knot

Half Knot

Hitches

Vertical Hitch

Half Diagonal Hitch

Loop Knot

Lark's Head Knots

Reverse Lark's Head Knot

Barrel Knot

Large Knot in Barrel

Spiral Knot

Mounting Knots

Overhand Knot

Gathering Knot

CHAPTER 3. BEGINNER'S GUIDE TO MACRAMÉ CORD SELECTION — 35

Macramé Cord Selection

Composition Macramé Cord

Texture Macramé Cord

Cord Size of Macramé

What Cord Are You Using for Macramé?

CHAPTER 4. TERMINOLOGY — 42

CHAPTER 5. TIPS IN SELECTING, MEASURING, AND KNOTTING YOUR MACRAMÉ CORDS — 48

Decorations and Useful Enhancements

CHAPTER 6. BEGINNING MACRAMÉ — 51

First: Training How to Perform Macramé

Macramé Practice Project

What Materials Do We Need for Macramé?

How Much Time Did Our Large Macramé Project Take?

CHAPTER 7. IMPORTANT THINGS TO REMEMBER AND FAQS — 61

Things to Remember

FAQs

CHAPTER 8. PROJECTS — 67

1. Macramé DIY Feathers
2. Wall Hanging DIY Bohemian Macramé Mirror
3. Hex-Nut Bracelet Macramé

4. Macramé Glass Connector Bracelet DIY

5. DIY Macramé Sunscreen Holder

6. Macramé Dip-Dyed Mobile

7. Knotted Chevron Headband

8. Giant Macramé Rope Lights

9. Hexagon Macramé Mug Coasters

10. DIY Macramé Rainbow

CHAPTER 9. PERSONAL PROJECTS 98

11. Macramé Braided Friendship Bracelet

12. Macramé Bottle Vases

13. DIY Macramé Plant Holder

14. Macramé Square Coasters

15. Jar Hanger

16. Hanging

17. Macramé Watch Band

18. Macramé Yarn Garland

19. Macramé Stone Necklaces

20. Macramé Laptop Mat

21. Macramé Dreamer

22. Macramé Table Runner

23. Plant Hanger With Ceramic Bowls

24. Macramé Umbrella Tassels

25. Macramé Blanket

26. Hanging Macramé Garden

27. Macramé Room Divider

28. DIY Hanging Macramé Chair

29. Macramé Play Tent

30. Macramé Placemat

31. Macramé Mason Jars

32. Macramé Rope and Dowel Planter

33. Macramé Spiral Bracelet

34. Openwork Macramé Bracelet

35. Macramé Rainbow Ornaments

36. Giant Agate Macramé Jewelry Pendant

37. Home Accent Macramé Rug

38. Wool and Yarn Macramé Wreath

39. Macramé Hanging—Half-Circle (Semi-Lunar)

CHAPTER 10: HOUSE PROJECTS — 183

40. Plant Hanger

41. Macramé Hanging Vase

CONCLUSION — 192

Introduction

Macramé is an aspect of decorative knots that permeates nearly any culture but can manifest in various forms. The practice of knot making is primarily practiced among the youth scouts and the cadets, particularly in the second cycle institution as part of their training sessions. Macramé art has become further widespread since its official presentation as a subject in different universities. It is now used in collaboration with other products to fashion all kinds of beautiful works of art. Due to its rapid growth, great adaptability, and comprehensive applications, macramé is strongly associated with trendy teens.

Regarding its use for fashion accessories, macramé is practiced in Eastern textiles and became a significant factor in creating each decorative garment, particularly at each tent, apparel, and towel fringes. In traditional ways, it became the most common textile technique. As time progressed, knots were used for several mnemonics, utilitarian, and superstitious reasons, and in Africa, knots were used in the fishnet and decorative fringes. Knotting originated in early Egyptian history. The Incas of Peru used the Quipu, built of the mnemonic knot (overhand knots), to record and convey information. The knots' use, the form of knots, the color of a cord, and the knot all helped report the complicated messages. In ancient Greece, knots have been used in medicine (as slings for the broken bones) and in sports, such as the Gordian knot, which was one such puzzle. The "Hercules" knot (square knot) with supernatural or religious connotations on clothes, jewelry, and pottery was used by early Egyptians and Greeks. Asmah (2005) reported that the strong interaction between the IRAI graduates and macramé led to discovering a range of methodologies and an integrative technology in the content and techniques adapted, particularly in most cases. As a result of the scholarly artisans' artistic touch, this human cultural accomplishment incorporated modern architecture requiring certain materials for trendy artifacts (Asmah, 2006). While macramé art has been developed and used for further production to achieve practical and aesthetic appeal in most cultures, its end products vary from one culture to another. The use of knotting for ornament distinguishes early cultures and represents intellectual growth. For all ages and abilities, it is a craft. Today, macramé is celebrating the Revival of the 20th century. Men and women turn to work with their hands and build utilitarian pieces and aesthetic ones. Despite the value of macramé, this flexibility and versatility present macramé as just a form knotting technique.

Macramé is full of vitality, adaptability, and exploratory, which lends itself in many ways to processing and handling in product creation and manufacturing. Since the very earliest days, macramé art has become an extremely valued skill around the world.

According to Asmah (2005), macramé development's journey passed through Arabia in the 13th century. During the Moorish conquest, spread to Turkey and Spain and to the rest of Europe in the early 14th century, arrived in Italy and France in the early 14th and 15th centuries, and was later adopted into England in the late 17th century and mid-to-late 19th century in the Victorian period. According to historians, sailors are said to have dispersed this style of art around the world. By the 1920s, macramé had reached its dormant period in China and America, making artifacts like flower hangers, skillfully fashioned bags, and industrial containers. Macramé has also proved to be a fantastic natural treatment for those undergoing recovery treatments and improves memory once again, making it an excellent experience for all. Playing with and tying the ropes will strengthen the hands and arms and helps loosen the wrist and finger joints. As it takes attention, it will also help relax the mind and spirit, and the repeated patterns put a weaver in the meditative mood. Also, tension through the fingers is assumed to be expelled, making macramé knotting a pleasant task. By establishing the intrinsic target concealed inside, macramé has the added advantage of loving the self-expression process.

Chapter 1
What Is Macramé?

For decades, macramé has been a common form of decorating, adding texture and comfort into a home/office with particular and unique knots that can be placed together in a creative way to make unique wall hangings, other decorations, plant holders, and more.

You are learning what is macramé because to build a macramé project, you need to know a handful of knots.

All you have to do is get your supplies and the equipment that you need and get familiarized with some specific macramé words you may need to know before you're ready to start learning how to macramé.

Here's what you need to know and have to make macramé knots:

- Macramé cord. Your macramé cord can be made of any material form of jute, cotton, hemp, plastic thread, twine, or chain. This comes in various shapes, shades, and turns.

- For support, you may need anything to attach your ties to. Standard options involve dowel rods, sticks, rings, or hoops.

- Clippers

To actually do it, you need to follow some instructions:

1. **Split rope and attach on the branch:**

    - I began cutting 20 bits of a 7-foot cord.

    - First, I tied the ties to the sycamore branch with the reverse lark's head knot.

    - Because the ropes were divided in half to fasten them to the limb,

I wound up with 40 lines dangling down at approximately 3 feet.

2. **Create a square triangle using knots:**

- I made a whole set of square knots on the very first row to do this.

- I left 2 on each side on the second row and then created square knots with the 36 ropes remaining.

- I kept leaving 2 more on each leg. So, I left 4 on each side on the 3rd row, leaving me with 3 sets of 2 ropes each left to make square knots.

- I kept going on until I had just 4 ropes left in the center to make the final square knot. I made 4 square knots at the bottom of the triangle.

- I then used a half-hitch knot, pulled diagonally, to construct the lines running along with the triangle.

Some Items to Gift to Your Friends

The following are a few items that you can do for yourself or for your mates using macramé:

- **Keychains:** You may offer the most beautiful and discreet present to a buddy they'll love! Nice practice for the latest abilities in macramé too!

- **Macramé feathers**: Trendy bohemian feathers are a perfect beginning macramé project for you to have fun making with friends!

- **Jar hanger**: This project is too simple to complete in only 5 minutes!

It is a great place to practice the ties first!

- **Garland with macramé**: A lovely garland constructed of carefully knotting macramé cord.

- **Feather earrings**: Easy, frilly feathered DIY earrings crafted from basic ties, and gorgeous

- colors of your choosing.

- **Macramé necklaces**: The macramé necklaces are extremely stunning and would make lovely presents and a really good piece for a night outside in town!

- **Plant hanger**: This is a basic macramé plant hanger project that you can create easily or try something fun and vibrant out of neutral twine!

- **Produce bag**: Lessen your waste when sporting to the general store with the latest customized macramé bag! Great for produce shopping!

- **Wristwatch band**: Offer your bet by making coordinating watches with crocheted bands for yourself and your best friend. It makes a nice and enjoyable present!

- **Zig-zag band**: Given the fact that this bracelet doesn't look so simple, to create it requires only 1 knot!

- **Coasters**: Elegant coasters that you should all macramé yourself! Nice for a table or perfect as presents!

- **Wall hanging**: This boho-chic DIY project blends beauty and purpose by making a stylish way to hang a mirror on the wall!

- **Cute earrings**: The DIY Earrings macramé is too new that I just have to make them the good! They'll look fantastic too, with beautifully colored lines!

- **Lens strap**: Try buying a fresh computer brace? Okay, don't buy it-do it! Your mates are going to be extremely jealous of the charm!

- **Headband-chevron**: It might be fun to tackle when you create and build a beautiful headband when learning your latest skills with your friend.

Macramé is as easy as only a couple of quick ties for keeping plants in your indoor room, a seasonal display, a fish tank, or something else you might get up with! Alternatively, it may get a bit complex with a different piece of macramé project on your board. You can also use this to jazz up a bland piece, attach a unique look to a pair of shoes, a headband, or just anything you want! When you have the feel of this newly learned talent, you'll tie up anything that your heart needs and apply macramé to your things!

Macramé is an enjoyable hobby and it can also be a perfect place to pass some good time with your friends while you chat, drink coffee, and make friendship bracelets for yourself!

Chapter 2
Basic Macramé Knots

Macramé things look pretty but still too complex and challenging to achieve. You will not believe it, but the architecture of most macramé plays is focused on the various combinations of a few simple knots! There is only a handful of these.

Here are just a few words you need to learn before you start:

- **Cord knotting.** This is the rope or collection of cords used to create the knot for a specified thread.

- **Knot-bearing string.** That is the rope or group of cords wound together by the knotting cords. In a macramé pattern, the knotting rope and the knot-bearing rope will shift step by step. For example, you are going to have a one-knot bearing rope while working the diagonal half hitch but there are going to be several knotting cords operating on the same knot-bearing cord one after the other.

- **Sennit.** This applies to a replicate worked sequence of the exact same thread. For instance, if you create 6 half knot stitches in a line then you are going to have a 6 half knots sennit.

When you get to know those knots, you can create virtually any project you want!

SQUARE KNOT

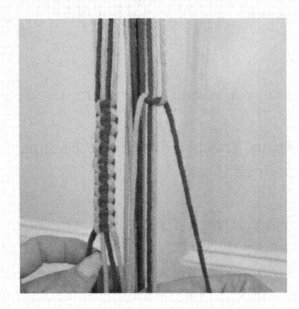

This knot consists of 2 flat ties, connected in different directions.

1. Install 2 threads and 4 ends can surface. Operating for the 2 side ends (operating cables), the foundation cables are 2 middle ones.

2. Place the left end above the threads in the middle, and the right end beneath them. You tied the flat knot only.

3. Now repeat step 1, but start with the right functioning thread.

4. Pulling at the ends tightens the strings. Here is the square knot!

HALF KNOT

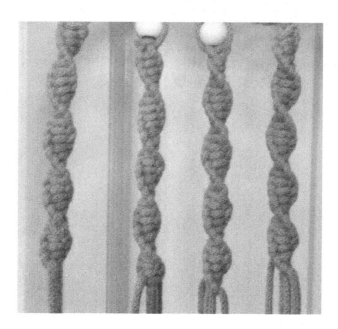

The half knot runs on 4 strings. The knotting strings are the 2 outer strings, and the knot-bearing strings are the 2 middle cables.

1. Place the left cord on the 2 knot-bearing strings to the north, and under the right knotting cable.

2. Place the knotting right strand to the left beneath the 2 knot-bearing strands and on the knotting left cable.

3. Pull a half-knot to hold. If you operate a half-knot sennit, they'll start spiraling naturally.

HITCHES

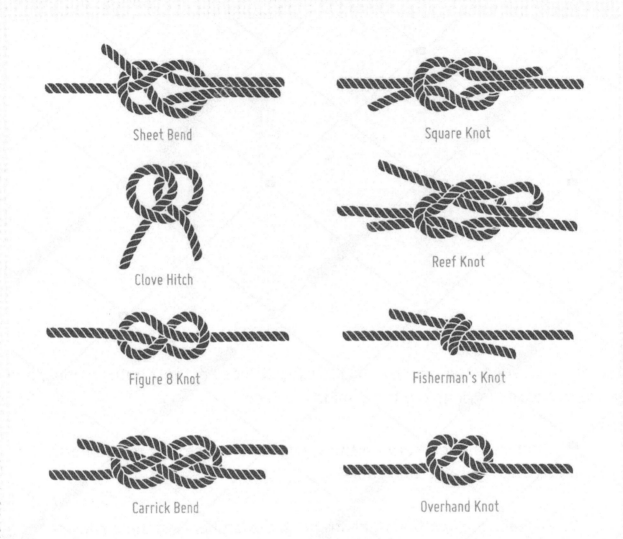

The hitches can be horizontal, longitudinal, or triangular (clove hop knot, clove knot). It depends on the base thread orientation (if you position it at an angle flat or diagonally).

Let's make the horizontal hitch starting:

1. Drag the left-hand side cord over the other cords to the opposite (that would be a reference thread).

2. Build the second chord with the double-half hook on it.

3. Instead attach the 3rd cord through the double-half hop, etc. It is a double-half hitch knot arrangement—the macramé big knot.

4. You'll get a horizontal hitch after you've attached every chord in a pair.

5. Again, through a flat edge cord above all other cords, as in step 1.

6. Create double-half hitches on the second side. You can reproduce it as much if you want. The hitch design is also commonly used for macramé.

7. When you position the base thread at such an angle, a diagonal hitch is produced which is somewhat close to the horizontal hitch.

VERTICAL HITCH

It is a form of hitches that tends to make a very thick job and is typically used to create ties, other items, and also carpets and wall decorations.

Source threads are located vertically.

1. Create a double-half hitch on each base rope-beginning from the left outermost cord (it will be our working rope which will be at least 6 times longer than that of the base threads).

2. Position the base thread often above the operating thread.

3. Go from left to right allowing dual half hitches.

4. Then move the other direction—right to left—and so on.

HALF DIAGONAL HITCH

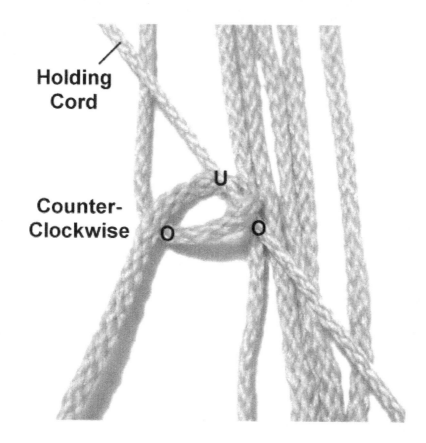

It is identical to the above horizontal half hitch. The distinction is that a knot-bearing rope is diagonally fixed until the knots are carried out. Below are the guidelines:

1. Bind the dowel to your cords. They are tied to the reverse larks head knot. For our case, the knot-bearing strand is going to be the left cord, and all the other wires will be wrapping cords.

2. Seal the bearing knot rope with a needle to the side of the cords.

3. Place your knot-bearing rope over the knotting strands at a diagonal.

4. Lock this to the right of your cords.

5. Begin with the knotting cord first (further to the left).

6. Loop it around and under your knot-bearing thread.

7. Using the same rope knotting. Lace it around the knot-bearing rope again, and then tie it into the connection that was formed between it. Zoom in to safety.

8. Follow the preceding 2 measures from the left to right for every knot-bearing thread, before you meet the diagonal edge.

That is a lateral half-line, left to right. You can also build a diagonal half hop. This is achieved by bringing into work the farthest right wire as your knot-bearing rope as well as the other strands as the knotting cables, working from right to left rather than left to right.

It will operate the same way for a horizontal half hitch except with your knot-bearing rope pinned horizontally around the item.

LOOP KNOT

Creating the loop knot is simple:

1. Only make a loop onto another string with one cable.

2. You will proceed to attach loops on the very same string, or by turns on both strings.

LARK'S HEAD KNOTS

Typically used to garnish the edges of macramé parts is the frivolité knot (sometimes named lark's head knot).

1. Next, add a thread to the foundation.

2. Then make a circle of the working cord around it, then draw the string under the base rope.

3. Create yet another coil, draw the rope over the base thread, and under the loop of the string. Tighten the tie.

Note: Work string is going up, down, under, up foundation cable. You should leave a small circle across every 2 lark's head knots and repair it with a screw. You'll get a frivolité picot.

REVERSE LARK'S HEAD KNOT

The reverse lark's head knot is performed opposite:

1. So, the hump is concealed in the back of your knot.

2. Split the rope in half and place the loop you just made under the dowel pin.

3. Take the coil around the front side and drag the 2 cords the stretch around the thread.

BARREL KNOT

This knot is also connected at tassel ends. This makes them tidy and customizable.

1. Create between 4–6 loops of chord finishing.

2. Push the top, then close the tie.

3. And break the knot beneath the extra yarn.

Large Knot in Barrel

Only lengthier (around 2 inches), identical to the previous knot. Good for finishing cord ends in things such as wall-hangings, hangers for plants, etc.

1. Stretch the rope in the manner that each end is at least 5 times greater than the length of the final knot—about 10 inches—to create a lovely long barrel knot.

2. Tie the longer end securely 7–10 times around both wires beginning from the tip.

3. Then bring the end downwards through to the ring.

4. So, tie the knot, push it upwards and pull it down gently (sliding motion).

5. That might need more work! Split off the extra thread.

SPIRAL KNOT

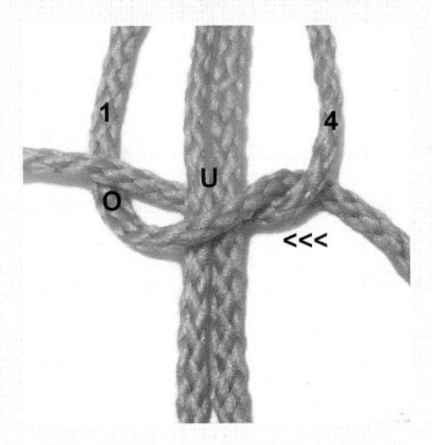

This produces a nice helix or loop of DNA. It is particularly well suited to be used when making hangers for plants. Also, this knot is a square knot but is repeatedly connected. The knot gets balanced, creating a spinning spiral.

1. Start by bending the working cord on the left, passing it over the filler cords, and under the right operational cord.

2. Move the right cord behind its filler strings, then drag it into the wrong working cord loop.

3. Pull softly on both strings.

4. Constantly repeat the above measures until the length you want is in the spiral.

MOUNTING KNOTS

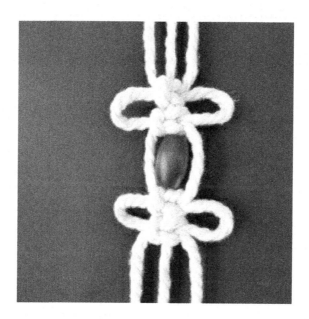

First of all, you will calculate the length of the yarn you'll use for your work. Here's a guideline (not rigid but useful): The thread duration must be around 4 times longer than the item you'd like to make. When you double the string, it needs to be 8 times longer. Yet then, the duration of the yarn relies on the nature of potential research (what knots are used, how many knots are used), and the thickness of the yarn (thicker thread-more weight).

1. Once the length of the yarn has been calculated, you can tie each thread to the pillow. The most popular way to do this is (doubled thread-making 2 ends), called the lark's head knot (frivolité knot).

2. You have to tie each thread independently, often. This form is classified as a double-half hitch. It can not only be used to install but also to build macramé. Or the simplest method of securing the thread: just fasten it with sticks! When you build a narrow macramé object (belt, necklace, etc.), the approach is fine.

3. And then, there's an example of decorative yarn stacking. Only attach a double-half hitch knot, make a loop, and then fix another double-half hitch knot.

OVERHAND KNOT

An overhand knot is a simple knot that ties together multiple cords. Different cables may be used, or even a single cable.

1. Stretch the string around a circle.

2. Move the ends of your strings to close around the coil.

GATHERING KNOT

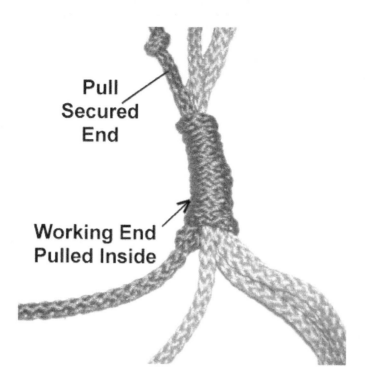

Also known as a wrapping knot, the gathering knot is a closure knot that binds cords together. You can also find these at the end of the plant hangers for macramé. This knot comprises 2 functioning strings; the remaining strings are going to work as filler cords. You need to take a different cord length (it is going to be your working cord) and build a lengthy loop (U-shaped) above the filler cord ring, with the loop facing downwards.

1. Beginning below the functioning cord's top-end—which points upwards—wrap it across your filler cords and your string. Make sure you keep the loop exposed for a while.

2. Move the wrapping string end into the loop on the bottom of your wrappings.

3. Pick up one end of your cord—that's stuck out upwards—that will put the rope under your wraps.

4. Draw through the wraps before the coil is enclosed.

5. The knot inset is complete!

6. To get a smooth finish, cut both ends of your working cord if you wish.

Chapter 3
Beginner's Guide to Macramé Cord Selection

A macramé cord comprises tangled or braided fibers/strands that bind or knot together to create a macramé recognized as a textile craft.

Most of you who are only starting will also read or hear either macramé yarn, strings, or rope referred to as macramé cord. Usually, the macramé cord has been used with such synonyms.

Macramé Cord Selection

It can be daring for new learners to realize what each term says, so let's dig further into the macramé cord and the numerous forms of cords you must know about. That way, for future projects, you can select the right cord.

We had no concept; there were various cord styles when we first began macramé. We thought it was just some plain-Jane string, and it's just required to create a macramé. We didn't know about all types of fibers for the projects that can be included. Little did we realize, not all macramé cords are produced similarly.

Let's have it broken down. The 3 different macramé cord styles include:

- Braided

- Single strand

- 3-ply / 3 strand

Any of the macramé projects would always fall under these types:

Braided Macramé Cord

Most beginners would start by buying a braided cord as it's the most inexpensive and simplest way to start macramé. Generally, several art shops and major box retailers sell braided cords. Whenever they want to start immediately, several people rush to their nearest shop to get any chord they might find. They would soon learn that a braided cord isn't the most appropriate thread for macramé making after finishing a few macramé projects.

The reasoning is that the braided string is simply a rope of cotton, polypropylene, polyester, nylon, or other sturdy fibers. It's cool to bind stuff together and offer it a firm grip, but it's hard to un-knot and fringe from it.

This isn't a poor place for getting started using a braided cord with all that already said. It gets the work finished, and you will wind up with the project that's decently accomplished. You will find yourself switching either with 3-ply— the most widely used macramé cord— or with the single-strand cord.

The usage of the macramé rope and cord can also be heard. Usually, they are arguing about a similar topic. We distinguish between the 2 because the thread is braided/3-ply cord typically and the cord is the all-encompassing phrase for fibers, yarn, and string.

Single Strand Macramé Cord

If you plan to get into macramé as a daily activity or full-time job, the single-strand cotton string is the best kind of macramé cord by far to pick from. Usually, the single-strand cord is more costly, but if you don't like to splurge on the expensive thread right now, find some inexpensive cotton string on amazon and begin with those. It's easy on the hand, and it's going to be nice to learn. It would make unraveling knots, tying knots, cutting the cord, and cord fringing far simpler.

3-Ply or 3-Stands Macramé Cord

The 3-ply is often pointed to as the cord of 3-stands. It consists of 3 smaller threads that shape a wide, twisted yarn. Macramé artists will also learn of utilizing 3-ply/4-ply macramé strings, which only implies the number of threads tied together to create a single cord strand.

That's what is known as multiply because you may get strands 4, 5, or 6 all twisted together to shape 1 strand until you begin moving through macramé strings that are far more than 3 strands. There are 4 strands tied together to create a single rope strand.

Now, as you know, the 3 macramé cord forms, let's explore 4 main points while choosing what macramé cord use for your macramé project and what you should search for.

Composition Macramé Cord

The composition of macramé rope breaks into 2 sections, synthetic or natural fibers.

- Fibers generated naturally in the atmosphere are natural fibers. Plants, organisms, or natural features create them. Cotton, jute, linen, hemp, and wool are examples of natural fibers. Every one of these fabrics can be broken down and reused naturally.

- Synthetic fibers are the other choice. Synthetic fibers are composed of tiny molecules from synthetic polymers. The substances used to produce these fabrics originate from raw resources, such as petrochemicals or chemicals based on petroleum. Nylon, spandex, and polyester are also other types of synthetic fibers.

Texture Macramé Cord

You can find that spool of cord seems to have a different feel, texture, and finish to it if you've seen a lot of macramé cords. It is a vital aspect of understanding the macramé cords to feel the various forms of cord texture.

The more macramé parts you create, the quicker you realize textures in all your macramé designs play a huge role.

If you are trying to make the purchase online on a macramé cord, try various brands to see what design suits you. You'll notice that not every cotton cords made of macramé are equal. The texture and feel of the threads can differ from manufacturer to manufacturer.

Cord Size of Macramé

When doing your ideal macramé project, understanding cord size is quite necessary. In the artistic presentation of macramé designs, the scale of the cord plays a key function.

On macramé cord sizes, we will not be moving into great depth.

Macramé cord is split down into 3 size groups for simplicity—small, medium, and large.

- **Small macramé cord.** Usually, the 1–2 mm. diameter cord. You can also see these strings utilized in creating jewelry to the thread by beads and buttons and small-detailed art projects.

- **Medium macramé cord.** Where most of all macramé designs are produced. Usually, it is from 3–5 mm. Quite commonly, 3–4 mm. will often go with you. Certain measurements are also used for lanterns, wall hangings, plant hangers, rugs, curtains, etc.

- **Large macramé cord.** These are the pieces of your macramé. This is going to be inside the range of something over 6 mm. These big sizes are typically used for covering broad space areas. The knots appear to be fewer, however, you can discover that they are still bigger.

What Cord Are You Using for Macramé?

The response is simple: it varies.

We would consider using the single-strand cotton cord of 3–4 mm. If you've tried some projects utilizing cheaper cords, and now you're happy investing in a nicer thread for projects of better quality, then you might be right with a single-strand cord. If you're a completely new user and would like to start using the correct thread directly, you should do it as well, by all means.

We would consider using a single-strand cord because it will increase our experience with macramé. Tying knots and unraveling them is going to be less of a battle. Cutting cords and fringing won't have to sound like hard work, and the macramé designs would be aesthetically appealing, most significantly.

Beginners in Macramé/Occasional Knotters

In our macramé path, we realize not everybody is at the same point, so our advice does not extend to everybody. We would consider using some rope that we have laid around to practice if we are new to this art. If not, if you're ready to start straight away, get some inexpensive cord from the nearest craft shop or grab some from Amazon. This Amazon cord is nicer than the thread that can be bought in the nearest craft shop—use this cord to learn tying ties, shapes, and series with macramé. To get you started, that's the cost-effective cord of macramé. To get a feel for creating the knots, begin to make smaller macramé crafts like keyrings or macramé feather designs.

Lovers and Enthusiasts of Macramé

We will suggest good quality 3–4 mm. single strand cotton cord for those looking to improve their macramé knotting skills and highlight their projects.

Alongside the uninterrupted fringing, knotting's smooth feel, and simplicity allow it to use the best kind of macramé cord. We will use this for 99 percent of our macramé projects.

The maximum macramé cotton cord is accessible online from Bochiknot Macramé. If you're trying to begin on macramé designs, there will be plenty of string to get you moving with one spindle of a 3 mm. single strand cotton cord.

2-3 mid-sized macramé projects should be done easily by one spool of macramé cord. If you're searching for only a little extra, 2 spools will be enough to cover the current and future macramé projects, so you don't run out of macramé string.

Chapter 4
Terminology

Of course, you could also expect that there are certain terms you would be dealing with while trying macramé out. By knowing these terms, it would be easier for you to make macramé projects. You will not have a hard time, and the crafting would be a breeze!

For this, you could keep the following in mind!

- **Alternating.** This is applied to patterns where more than 1 cord is being tied together. It involves switching and looping, just like the half-stitch.

- **Adjacent.** These are knots or cords that rest next to one another.

- **Alternating square knots (ASK).** You will find this in most macramé patterns. As the name suggests, it is all about square knots that alternate on a fabric.

- **Bar.** When a distinct area is raised in the pattern, it means that you have created a "bar." This could either be diagonal, horizontal, or vertical.

- **Bangle.** A bangle is any design with a continuous pattern.

- **Band.** It is a design that has been knotted to be flat or wide.

- **Buttonhole (BH).** This is another name given to the crown or lark's head knot. It has been used since the Victorian Era.

- **Button knot.** This is a knot that is firm and round.

- **Bundle.** These are cords that have been grouped as one. They could be held together by a knot.

- **Braided cord.** These are materials with individual fibers that are grouped as one. It is also stronger than most materials because all the fibers work together as one.

- **Braid.** Sometimes called a plait, this describes 3 or more cords that have been woven under or over each other.

- **Crook.** This is just the part of the loop that has been curved and situated near the crossing point.

- **Core**. This term refers to a group of cords that are running along the center of a knot. They are also called filling cords.

- **Cord.** This could either be the material or cord/thread that you are using, or specific cords that have been designed to work together.

- **Combination knot.** These are 2 knots that have been designed to work as 1.

- **Cloisonné.** It is a bead, with metal filaments, that is used for decorative purposes.

- **Chinese crown knot.** This is usually used for Asian-inspired jewelry or décor.

- **Charm.** This is a small bead that is meant to dangle and is usually just 1 inch in size.

- **Doubled.** These are patterns that have been repeated in a single pattern.

- **Double-half-hitch (DHH).** This is a specific type of knot that is not used in a lot of crafts, except for in really decorative, unusual ones. This is made by making sure that 2 half-hitches are resting beside each other.

- **Diameter.** This describes the material's weight, based on millimeters.

- **Diagonal.** This is a row of knots or a cord that runs from the upper left side to the opposite side.

- **Excess material.** This describes the part of the thread that is left hanging after you have knotted the fabric. Sometimes, it is hidden using fringes, too.

- **Fusion knots.** This starts with a knot so you could make a new design.

- **Fringe.** This is a technique that allows cords to dangle down with individual fibers, that unravel along the length of the pattern.

- **Flax linen.** This is a material derived from linseed oil that is best used for making jewelry and even macramé clothing. It has been used for over 5,000 years.

- **Finishing knot.** This is a kind of knot that allows specific knots to be tied to the cords, so they

- do not unravel.

- **Findings.** These are closures for necklaces or other types of jewelry.

- **Gemstone chips.** This is the term given to semi-precious stones that are used to decorate or embellish your macramé projects. The best ones are usually quartz, jade, and turquoise.

- **Horizontal.** This is a design of the cord that works from left to right.

- **Holding cord.** This is the cord to which the working cords are attached.

- **Hitch.** This is used to attach cords to other cords, dowels, or rings.

- **Inverted.** This means that you are working on something upside-down.

- **Interlace.** This is a pattern that could be woven or intertwined so that different areas could be linked together.

- **Micro-macramé.** This is the term given to macramé projects that are quite small.

- **Metallic.** These are materials that resemble silver, brass, or gold.

- **Mount.** To mount or mounting means that you have to attach a cord to a frame, dowel, or ring. This is usually done at the start of a project.

- **Netting.** This is a process of knotting that describes knots formed between open rows of space. It is usually used in wall hangings, curtains, and hammocks.

- **Natural.** These are materials made from plants or plant-based materials. Examples include hemp, jude, and flax.

- **Organize.** This is another term given to cords that have been collected or grouped as one.

- **Picot.** These are loops that go through the edge of what you have knotted.

- **Pendant**. A décor that you could add to a necklace or choker and can easily fit through the loops.

- **Synthetic.** This means that the material you are using is man-made and is definitely not natural.

- **Symmetry**. This means that the knots are balanced.

- **Standing end.** This is the end of the cord that you have secured, so the knot can be properly constructed.

- **Texture.** This describes how the cord feels like in your hand.

- **Tension or taut.** This is the term given to holding cords that have been secured or pulled straight so that they would be tighter than the other working cords.

- **Vertical**. This describes knots that have been knitted upwards, or in a vertical manner.

- **Working end.** This is the part of the cord that is used to construct the knot.

- **Weave.** This is the process of letting the cords move, as you let them pass over several segments in your pattern.

Chapter 5
Tips in Selecting, Measuring, and Knotting Your Macramé Cords

Learn how to buy the right type of macramé, measure the right amount of cord you want to use, and tie the strings correctly to create the right macro pattern. Designing too strong or too loose knots or wires, that are not aesthetically pleasing, will undoubtedly affect the appearance of the finished piece.

If you find that you no longer have a cable to work on or have too much cable left, you will know how important these tips are.

The most important tip to remember is to choose the right thickness when buying a macramé cord, as it is the deciding factor. A thicker cable requires a longer length; a pattern with many knots also requires a longer cable.

If you decide to use a different cable type than the recommended type in the pattern, you risk an outcome that you may not like. However, if you have sufficient experience with macramé cables, you can change cable types, as long as they have the required quantity, diameter, flexibility, structure, and strength.

If you decide to use a thicker cord than as shown in the pattern, be aware that you will need to create fewer knots than recommended in the pattern.

A thicker thread and lots of knots can make the piece uncomfortable, even if you use decorative accessories such as beads and pendants.

You should also be careful how you tie the knots tightly or loosely. Consistency is essential when creating a pattern. Strips that are too tight will stick together. They are not in the correct position to create the desired effect.

If you are still out of the thread, which happens to the best of us, there is always a method of splashing water that we can go back to. This is an emergency when the cord is stretched by cutting the cord in half lengthwise and then joining the 2 ends together by loosening the wires and covering them with a robust and transparent adhesive. Twist them together and allow them to air dry.

When choosing which product to use for a project, it is essential to think of what the finished piece will be, as well as exactly how it will be made use of, as some cords will be much more suitable for some projects. Frequently, stiff thick cords are not the best selection for making jewelry. However, they could be excellent for a shopping bag that will need to lug some weight and not battle royal or use it easily. If numerous kinds of cord would be suitable for a job, they might cause somewhat different completed products.

Decorations and Useful Enhancements

Grains are usually included in embellishment items used for macramé. Again, the ones you selected will undoubtedly need to be ideal for the cord being utilized, and also fit the function of the completed piece. Wooden grains are a perfect option; however, there is no reason why any other kind of hole, big enough to suit cords, should not be made use of. Various other products such as switches, sequins, and charms can additionally be utilized.

When making several kinds of items, a search for other items may be needed to finish the design. Instances of things that you might make use of are ear cords, clasps, buckles, break hooks, split rings, bamboo rings, and also switches.

Chapter 6
Beginning Macramé

There are enormous ways to seek a new skill or art. We aren't going to pretend to be a macramé professional. We'll take you on our personal experience and teach you how to do this from a newbie to the other.

To find one's own way to enjoy the enjoyable art of macramé, we're going to have all the tools you need. The cool thing is that you don't have to be a professional to make pretty decoration items for your house. It seems tough than it is. Let's get to it, then.

First: Training How to Perform Macramé

First, why should you start practicing? About how much? Our first "real project" cost about $30 for macramé rope (macramé cord, as sometimes it is referred) and a few dollars for wooden dowel.

Furthermore, you can't sprint down to Michael's or Hobby Lobby and get a macramé rope or the macramé cord. So, if you are like us and you like to initiate a project day when you say, "We want to begin this to ourselves," our advice is to start with a practice project as we did.

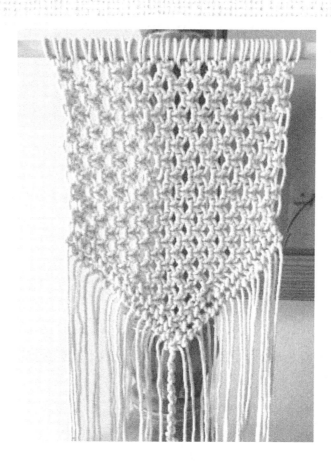

Macramé Practice Project

Reasons We Recommend the Small "Practice" Project

- When you are waiting for the macramé rope, it fills the time gap.

- This will offer you the ability to get acquainted with different types of macramé knots, their names, and how to do them.

- You will be very satisfied and completely prepared to go bigger on completing your practice assignment, or you will know that this is just not for you.

- Completing this practice project would give you the courage to spend your time and resources on the first "real" macramé project to take the next step.

What Macramé Project Should We Do?

Decide which project you would like to make. Look at web images of macramé.

What Kinds of Macramé Projects Can We Make?

Start from small projects such as:

- Book mark

- Jewelry including choker necklaces or bracelets keychain

- Plant holder

- Wall hanging

Bigger projects include:

- Table runner rug

- Light fixture headboard

- Hammock (save a big project like this for later) garland or bunting

Here are some steps you should follow to help you decide:

1. Decide on the form of the project. The 2 common starter projects involve wall hangings and plant holders.

2. Where's it heading? It will help decide what scale you want to build.

3. Look for a theme that relates to you. With the clean lines and readily established patterns, more unrestricted, and the organic or symmetric?

Where Do We Find Macramé Patterns?

You're able to seek a pattern after defining what sort of project or what theme appeals to you. On Etsy, we find our pattern for under $5. You're not going to purchase a pattern. Top 3 reasons we choose to purchase a pattern are:

- We looked at Etsy to get ideas on what sort of project we desired to make and discovered at that stage that it was an opportunity to purchase patterns. We've fallen in love with the project. That's just what we expected.

- Patterns are a very cheap alternative ($5–10).

- We enjoyed the thought of not doing work side-by-side with a recording, continuously halting and starting it. It seemed more relaxing for us to stay away from our computers.

What Macramé Pattern Did We Use?

People ask me about our unique trend. It's named "Four of Diamonds" from Reform Fibers if you want to restrict your search and are already interested in this pattern. On Etsy, you can search for their designs.

What Materials Do We Need for Macramé?

You'll know the amount of rope to buy until you have the project/pattern. We decided that we wanted to use a natural cotton rope, but when you pick your color and materials, you can have your particular taste and style. On Etsy, they sell cords (or rope). Nevertheless, the quantity or price we wanted was not available. Here is the connection we used after a lot of digging, our macramé project needed:

- 220 feet of 1/4 inches (6 mm.) of 3 strands of cotton rope to give you an idea

- Wood or the metal dowel, or a similar tree branch or drif2od (for an even more organic natural appearance), if you're doing wall art

- Scissors

- Tape measurement

- Tape (we used easily removable painters' tape)

- You can "seal" the ends by heating the ends with the candle flame as an alternative if you don't want to use tape.

- Rolling rack for dresses (or alternative method for the hanging project)

How Much Time Did Our Large Macramé Project Take?

This largely depends on the project you chose, but the actual work lasted about 2 1/2 hours for us. It took almost 3 hours to check the knots.

Can We Do This?

Yes, we're here to reassure you that it's possible. Here's a little confession of our experience:

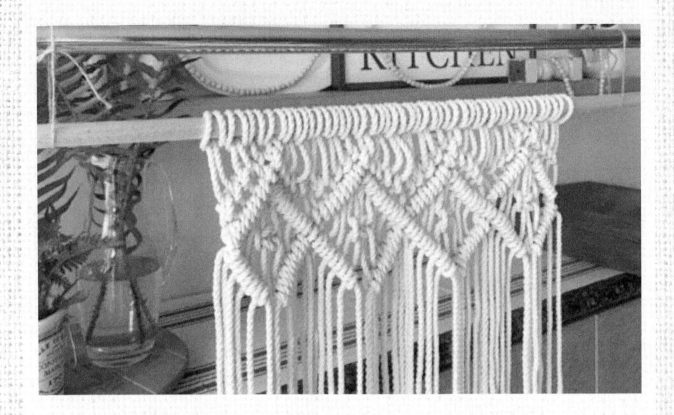

Confession No. 1

We never really had the diagonal clove hitch-knot on our first project. No matter what we did. We constantly pulled out the whole row and began a new about 3 times. We eventually wanted to let go of it.

My theory was that this stitch didn't apply itself well to the short string we were dealing with. It wasn't the same. Guess what? We are right. Hitch-knot (diagonal clove) looked just like the image as soon as we began working with the wider cord. What is the lesson? Friend, don't give up.

Confession No. 2

For the first time, we looked at the pattern; it seemed as if we were reading a Chinese article. There's no reason to worry. Do you know what we've been saying? You can do that. Do what we've been doing. That's how you're going to make it through.

When you take these things step by step and then keep track of the steps you are on, it's not complicated. We made the only mistake (we had to pull out a whole row) because we were a little too loose and didn't pay enough concentration to the step-by-step method.

Confession No. 3

Don't panic if you miss all the knots in your practice project that you thought you already know. If we did it, you can do it as well.

Options for the Hanging Your Project of Macramé While Working

- We described a "rolling clothing rack" undersupplies. We utilized this and what was suggested, but if you don't already own one, it's pricey and not required. You can function with your dowel or the ring hanging from comfortable somewhere.

- To protect the piece, you can hang this from a doorknob, the drawer knob, or anywhere you may find it.

- Using a suction cup hook or wreath hanger (over-the-door) are other suggestions.

- You can also (temporarily) pull down the piece of the art hanging on the wall and hang out your piece from the nail.

Chapter 7
Important Things to Remember and FAQs

Macramé's retro craftsmanship project has many surprising components and stunning modifications. You ought to adopt the proper strategies and procedures to practice this art or hone your talents.

For an outdoor and indoor product or item, there are several ways to start a project. Here are some excellent ideas that will help to make the best of your art.

Things to Remember

Practice the skill

Practice your abilities to prevent needless failures down the path before you begin to make anything. Remember, having the project going will cost you several bucks. It contains the costs you may need for equipment and accessories.

So, you can begin with a smaller practice project to improve your abilities for a bigger one instead of spending these efforts on failed attempts. It can familiarize you with numerous knots as well as designs.

Invest in a Fiber of High-Quality

The fiber's choice is by far the most important phase in the process before beginning your project. Choose the proper fiber form that may contain cords, strings, yarn, or ropes. In this range, the fiber material means the most. Cotton, jute, hemp, nylon, etc., are the options used.

For beginner-level designs, experts often consider utilizing cotton cords with just a diameter of 3 mm. To help the project, it is not only versatile and adjustable but also gentle and durable. There are also cotton ropes available in 2 varieties, viz—twisted and braided cords. For your project, select the thread that fits.

Maintain Sufficient Tension

You will become a specialist in the handling of a macramé project with the necessary experience. Here the force used to strengthen the knots will mainly impact the final performance. It may even spoil other elements' consistency.

So, for consistent knotting, it makes much more sense to perform the proper amount of stress you like. If the knots in areas seem shoddy, you can need to find the appropriate combination between tightening them and loosening them.

Select Easy Patterns

Start with a basic pattern to build your masterpiece, whether working on a starter or middle-level design. It may be a plain square knot or an alternate square knot.

There are simple, easy ways to make patterns. In these models, you will learn to maintain uniformity. It would be best if you also used the independent boards or anchoring strategies to hold the work-in-progress stable in place.

Use the Right Amount of Rope

The number of ropes you require is 5–6 times the completed item's total length. Still hold the tip of an additional cord length at the bottom of the thing to create fringes and other decorative accents. You do not want a short rope, as it will thoroughly spoil your project.

Even attaching ropes, later on, is tough. Around the same moment, though, there's still no reason to waste the remaining strings. You may do smaller projects for the shorter cords, such as jewelry, bookmarks, or key chains.

FAQs

Can Macramé Be Washed?

Yes! Macramé is very stable and does not readily fall apart. In a tiny garment bag, it can be a machine, washed at 86°F. Only hang to dry.

Can You Use Yarn to Macramé?

Yes! It's possible to use yarn. You can realize that only the scale of macramé knots would be as wide as the thread or substance you are using. The smaller your choice of string, yarn, or cord, the smaller the knots would be. The loops would not be very clear if the thread is too thin. Instead of a bigger project like a wall hanging, yarn may be perfectly adjusted to the micro-macramé project to be used in jewelry making, for example.

Can You Macramé With Jute?

Yes! Macramé artists used jute and hemp popularly, but the lack of consumer demand led to nylon and the satin rayon macramé cords, and other human-made fibers. Nylon cords or cotton are preferred for beginners because, in the event of an error, they are simple to unravel.

How to Choose What Sort of Macramé Cord to Utilized for Our Project?

When choosing your content, there are several things to consider. There's always something apparent to consider availability and cost. But with your idea, you will also want to understand the strength of the content. For example, if you want to hang a vine, you want to use a stronger rope, such as those made of jute, ribbon, leather, nylon, or cotton.

Furthermore, you should consider a cord's stiffness. You would want to use shorter, more lightweight cords for jewelry, such as a cotton embroidery cord that is very smooth and flexible. When creating an outdoor project, you may want to use a sturdy and long-lasting polypropylene chain, either the outdoor plant keeper or an outdoor hammock.

What Size Cord Should We Use?

You would want to select the thickness of 4.0 mm. or more for the larger decorations like wall hangings or plant holders, depending on the project. You can use a cord shorter than 2.0 mm. in diameter for the smaller micro-macramé designs, such as bracelets and necklaces.

How Much Cord Do We Need for Macramé?

The cords you will use for knotting would need to be between 5–6 times the length of the completed one. The cords that are your "core" cords used for the form, but that are not necessarily knotted may just need to be around twice the final length. For having a fringe or the other decorative attachments at the ends, note to leave additional cord length. And rather than too little, it's better to have much rope. At the top, you can still trim lengthy bits.

How Do We Keep Our Knots Looking Uniform?

The easiest way to ensure that the knots are uniform, to make certain that the friction on your cords is kept equally and that every knot lines up straight, vertically, horizontally, and diagonally on both sides. You would want to check and knot, particularly when you are only learning, confirm that its lines with the proceeding knot edges are strong and that the loops are even. The only way to make sure that the project is successful is to protect the project. You'll like to hang it from the clothes rack or a safe hook for larger ventures. Ideally, you can hang from 2 points on the project so that the project does not rock back and forth. You'll like to make a macramé board for smaller projects like jewelry ones.

What Is the Macramé Board?

The macramé board is a location where you protect your knitting project. This can be created from several different materials, but you essentially want to make a firm surface where you can insert pins. A corkboard, a sheet of polyurethane, or the 2 pieces of cardboard bound together may be used. Without poking out the other side, the board should be around 12 inches square and thick to put a T pin or the corsage pin in.

Why Is Macramé Getting Back?

Macramé was popular with the hippie movement back in the 1970s, but as a part of the latest tribal and the Boho (Bohemian) style trends in home decor, it has moved back into fashion.

Where Did Macramé Originate?

Macramé is believed to derive from the Arabic term "migramah," meaning fringe, which corresponds to the custom of the 13th century used by Arab weavers for decorating the fringes on the camels and the horses to keep animals safe from the flies.

It can also come from a Turkish word for napkin or towel, meaning "makrama." Macramé was used as a means to protect the loomed fabrics' lower edges. Macramé's first known uses occurred in Babylonians and Assyrians' decorative carvings.

Macramé was most common in the Victorian period, where most homes were decorated with this art in products such as bedspreads, tablecloths, and curtains. Queen Mary also taught her ladies-in-waiting macramé in the 17th century. In the 19th century, Macramé was also a favorite pastime of the British and the American sailors who made tiny crafts that they either sold or exchanged in port.

Chapter 8
Projects

1. MACRAMÉ DIY FEATHERS

As of late, lovely, feathery macramé feathers have clogged up our social ne2rking accounts—but we are not upset about it. They are incredibly beautiful, and we certainly find ourselves bookmarking them saved to buy, to hang out in the children's room. But we were also interested, of course, to see how they were crafted. How are you getting the wonderfully soft fringe in the world? Okay, we finally got the answers, and that requires a cat brush. Said plenty. However, frankly, the options here are limitless, and we can't wait to watch more of this method. But we think we'll encourage you to create these at home in the meanwhile.

Materials

- Cat brush

- 5 mm. single twist cotton string

- Sharp fabric shears

- Ruler

- Fabric stiffener

- For a med sized feather, cut:

    o 1 piece of strand for the spine (32 inches)

    o 10-12 pieces of strands for the top (14 inches)

    o 8-10 pieces of strands for the middle (12 inches)

    o 6-8 pieces of strands for the bottom (10 inches)

Instructions

1. Fold in half the 32 inches strand. Taking 1 of several 14 inches strands, fold it in half, then under the spine strap it.

2. Take another 14 inches strand, bend it in half and place it into the top straight strand loop. Drag it across and put it on top of the opposite strand horizontally.

3. Now via the top string, draw the lower strands all the way. This's

your tie.

4. Tightly pull both ends. You'll rotate the beginning side to the next row. So, if you first place the horizontal strand from the left side to the right side, you will place the next horizontal strand from the right side to the left side.

5. Lie underneath the spine of the first bent strand, insert the folded strand into its loop. Drag the top circle thru the lower strands. Then tighten.

6. Keep on working and function down in scale steadily.

7. Force the strands up to strengthen—catch the base of the center (spine) strand of one hand and move the strands up with the other hand. Pull the fringe back to reach the bottom of the center strand until you're finished.

8. Could you give it a rugged finish, then? That does not only serve to direct the form but also helps to smooth the strands out. To be real, the smaller the strands, the better. It also helps to get a very keen pair of fabric shears.

9. Put the feather on a sturdy surface after a harsh scrub since you can need an animal brush to brush off the cording. The brush can destroy every weak or wood layer, so we consider using a slicing mat for self-healing or perhaps a flat piece of cardboard.

10. Begin at the spine while brushing and press deep into the string when brushing. To get the perfect, smooth fringe, it'll take many hard strokes.

11. Make your way back. Keep the spine's base while brushing when

you're at the bottom. You wouldn't want the brush to pull some strands off.

12. Next, the feather will be stiffened. The stitch is so delicate that if they pick that up and decide and place it, it will only flop. Offer it a spray, then take at least a couple of hours to start.

13. You may also go back to give it a last scrub after the feather has stiffened up a little. This, we'd imagine, is the most difficult step. Take it simple. It's easier to cut less than more. And founded on how much you move the item, you will need to change the trim. After you're finished cutting, for good measure, you may also give this another strip of fabric stiffener.

2. WALL HANGING DIY BOHEMIAN MACRAMÉ MIRROR

Materials

- Cording macramé of 4 mm.
- Sharp Scissors (also available at JoAnn Fabrics)
- Ring of wood of 2 inches

- Wood beads of 25 mm., hole size of 10 mm.

Instructions

1. Split the 4 bits of macramé cord into parts of 108 inches.

2. Fold the pieces in half and use a lark's head knot to attach all 4 of them into the wood ring. Drag the knots around each other firmly and closely. Split and begin tying 2 of the lark's head ties into some kind of square knot.

3. Begin to attach 2 square knots into another 2 additional lark's head knots.

4. As you begin the 2nd square knot string, merge them into one big broad square knot from one of the other 2 square knots' edges.

5. Tie 7 square knots moving down each side and totally.

6. After binding the knots, cut off the ends. 2 strings on either line or 4 strings in the center. To cover the split ends, apply tape to the endpoints of the cord. This would make the beads simpler to add. Congratulations. This has been the tough part. The remainder is only tying simple knots and also having the ends.

7. Attach 1 bead to every one of the rows of the 2-side cords. Tie a string from both sides underneath the bead, rendering it even. Tie the middle of the 4 cords into a single or (overhand knot) around 1/14 inches well below beads.

8. From the middle, take 1 cord and connect this to the 2 cords on the ends. Tie the 3 around each other from both sides in a knot. To get even knot sizes, attach the mirror. To keep it still, apply one of its 3-side cords

to the backend of the mirror.

9. On the lower left and right of the mirror, tie easy knots into all 3-side cords. Split the 3-side cords again. Place one on either side of the mirror's back to keep 2 across each side of the mirror's front and bind it into a knot.

10. Switch the mirror over and tie together all the strings. Switch the mirror back across the front tie and undo it. Within the tie, slip the back cords and strengthen the knot. Cut the end of the chord downwards to around 14 inches. Pull the edges or loosen the cording, then cause them to fray. Brush the edges of the string with the edges of the brush to fluff. Hang it and enjoy it.

3. HEX-NUT BRACELET MACRAMÉ

The bracelet we are creating is a little different from the "braided hex-nut bracelet" but rather uses macramé, which would be perfect, because a little ago we vowed some guides and felt a little sad we had not already written some so far.

Remember: We used multiple-colored cords in the tutorial to make things simpler for you to find out what was going on.

Materials

- 4 string sizes only for a hex-nut bracelet, every measuring around 60 cm. in total

- 1 piece of hex-nut

Instructions

1. Knot together 4 cords.

2. Over the middle 2 strings, put the left cord. Then beneath the middle 2 cords and into the left cord's loop, put the right cord over the left cord. Pull that cord left then right before the knot hardens.

3. Over the middle 2 cords, put the right cord. Then beneath the middle 2 cords and into the loop created by the right cord, put the right cord over the right cord. Push the rope left then right before the knot hardens. Yay. A square knot has been tied.

4. If you choose a bead (or hex-nut) to be added, thread it into the middle 2 cords and then keep on creating square knots.

5. This may appear a bit difficult at first, but after you've done it many times, We guarantee that you'll be sorted out.

4. MACRAMÉ GLASS CONNECTOR BRACELET DIY

Everyone loves bracelets made of macramé. But what we love most is creating them. Something here is so soothing about tying knots. Only do so if you have not tried it. We have added few glass connectors in vivid colors this time around, and these look so stylish. Here are some step-by-step guidelines for 2 separate methods of producing them.

Materials

- 3 m. of string—We will use a 2 mm. cord, but you might choose a 1-millimeter cord (but strongly recommend at least 1.5 mm. to make it more durable). You could use a macramé cord (should not use wax cord) or other cord forms as far as it can be burnt.

- Glass connections

Instructions

1. Cut 2 bits out of approx. 20 cm. or 2 bits each of 1 m.

2. Let us just design a "spiral" bracelet initially. Taking your 20 cm.

part and slip it into your connector on 1 side.

3.   Taking your 1-meter piece and connect in the center with a knot. Now you've got 2 cords, one from the left, one from the right.

4.   Take the correct cord and slip it above the left cord under the center cord.

5.   Taking the left chord now, slipping it down over the center cords, and making a knot underneath the left cord.

6.   Repeat such steps before you create a bracelet on one side. To complete it, split the endings off and burn them to melt and stitch in position. Then take its other side. A spiral would be formed when you tie your knots.

On with the second technique now:

1.   Steps 1, 2, and 3 were like the first one with this technique.

2.   The change is that you're not making the same move again and again now. Instead, slip the left cord underneath the center cords and then over the right and right cords over-center cords and underneath the left cord after tying the first knot.

3.   Tie a knot even with 2 knots.

4.   Tie knots variously around each side before you meet the target length. For the opposite side of a bracelet, repeat.

5.   Keep the bracelets flexible rather than a clasp, utilizing one smaller bit of cord and the second process. Only pull the 2 ends together and bind the knots upon these 2 ends.

6.

5. DIY MACRAMÉ SUNSCREEN HOLDER

We purchased a sunscreen tube last summer with such a carabiner that we hooked on to our bag. It continued all summer and was almost the greatest discovery of all time.

We rarely forgot the sunscreen again because without needing to search around in our bag, we can re-apply on the way. We misplaced the convenient travel sunscreen this summer, so we decided to replicate it. We will design this cute and inexpensive DIY macramé sunscreen carrier because we like macramé so much. You can use it to bear hand sanitizer and lotion as well.

Materials

- Tape
- Carabiner
- Scissors
- Small empty jar
- Candle
- Sunscreen
- String

Instructions

1. Slice 5-string parts about 20 inches long.

2. Fold it up and tie it in the center of one large knit. To secure it in position, tape the knot down.

3. Break the string into 5 pairs and knot around 1 inch down each pair. Another 1 inch down now, pick one string, then knot it next to it with the string from the set.

4. Follow this for around 4 rows of knots and to cover the size of your bottle. To test the match and numbers of knots required, slip your bottle inside. For easier usage, we will place the bottle upside down in the cap.

5. Tie a large knot for all strands to keep the jar in place until the fit is

correct.

6.	Position each bit of string over the flame to melt the edges to stop fraying.

7.	To end, tie the top knot to the carabiner and connect it to your bag.

8.	All summer last year the travel-sized bottle was sufficient for us, but you may refill it as desired. You won't have to search through your bag now anytime you want a little sunscreen control. Summer, happy.

6. MACRAMÉ DIP-DYED MOBILE

Breathe fresh life with this simple bohemian-inspired mobile into an old-school macramé.

Materials

- 10 inches hoop embroidery

- Scissors

- White twine

- Aquatic water

- Wide bowl

- Handicraft stick

- Fabric paint

- Bag for garbage

- Elastic ribbon

Instructions

1. Remove the outside bracket from the hoop for embroidery. Split into 90 bits of twine of various lengths (no shorter than 12 inches). Fold any single piece in half. Put any folded piece under, over, then pull to lock the ends via the loop.

2. Collect hung twine in 4-strand bunches. Knot together to protect the embroidery hoop 1/2 inch below. Repeat across the hoop the entire time.

3. Grab 2 sets of the first bunch of twine and knot with 2 pieces of the 2nd bunch of twine 1/2 inch below the first row of knots. Repeat across the hoop the entire time.

4. Using a craft stick to combine 3 tsps. fabric paint with 3 cups of lukewarm water in a wide tub. Gather the hanging twine and the stable midway elastic. For 30 minutes, soak the ends of the elastic bands in the paint-water solution. Place it on a plastic waste bag to dry for 24 hours. Remove the outer embroidery hoop, elastic and stable.

7. KNOTTED CHEVRON HEADBAND

If you have piled this many bracelets as you can probably put on your wrists and are not prepared to avoid knotting, these headbands are for you. It's only an extremely large bracelet of friendship adjusted to rest perfectly on top of your head. We will pick bright sherbet colors and gray overtones. However, you realize that the stunning possible variations continue for days if you've stared at a show of sewing floss.

Materials

- Embroidery floss (6 colors 12 strands to match our ½ inch square headband)

- Thick satin ribbon (1/8–1/4 inch is fine)

- E6000 or comparable adhesive that adheres to plastic

- Large headband of your choice (1/2 inch)

- Similar stitching thread needle

- Our head cannot fit headbands that attach or elastic into position, so we use rubber. We finished spending the entire day adjusting them. We are confident you can change this to fit your tastes if you want a particular theme.

Instructions

1. Begin by having your friendship bracelet super long.

2. We will use 6 strands that are 10 feet long each, folded up to be 5 feet long. However, your strands can be longer if the headband is broader.

3. Keep the strands connected, attach a temporary knot, and function on the traditional friendship bracelet until the strip is around 1 1/2 inches smaller than the headband duration.

4. Untangle the knot once you are done.

5. Place on the headband's backside a mark of adhesive then winds the ribbon around the headband. Be sure you align the ribbon on the frontside and backside, and so the better side is out if the satin ribbon is just a single face. Before proceeding, let this set up for a few minutes.

6. From one side of the knotted string, cut the tail off and glue them down. Again after a few minutes, let everything set up.

7. Place the adhesive on the back and tie the ribbon across the tangled strip, so all that is imperfect is hidden. And begin gluing and binding.

8. Since you're at the same length from this side as you were all from the other, avoid gluing and covering.

9. At this point, cut the tails, then glue along the entire length of a pretty long bracelet. You're going to have to spread it a bit to fit in, and that's fine. Hold the back and cover around the strip's edges before the end of the headband is hit and the end of the ribbon is neatly glued to the back.

10. You should stitch backward and forwards around the back at this stage if you have just glued the top, grabbing the sides of the knotted section and pulling it firmly into place. This is a fine option of very uneven edges for the strip.

8. GIANT MACRAMÉ ROPE LIGHTS

So, when we say giant, we are talking about huge. Not just the rope, but also the light bulbs.

For this project, the knot is as basic as it can be. It's a perfect way to be active to stream Netflix, so you can kind of go on autopilot until your hands have the memory down.

Materials

- Rope/cording (be sure that a voucher is used.)—Do not throw stuff at me, but we don't know how much rope to say you to get. Only let me elaborate. We bought 35 yards ($1.49/yard) for the enormous rope, and it filled 15 feet of lamp cord comfortably. We bought 40 m. ($0.59/yard) for the smaller one, which protected 8 feet. The thickness certainly plays a great role in how far it travels. If you need to incorporate more and you will never see them, the good news is that you can use transparent tape to tie the ends together (also make sure that you use at least a 40 percent off coupon at JoAnn when you are buying it.)

- Cord of lamp

- Kit socket

- Small Vessel

Instructions

1. Start by securing the wire for your lamp. You'll want to loop it around things like a chair back or doorknob in real life to hold it steady for photos we have taped to a wall.

2. Find the middle of your cord and put it behind the wire of your lamp. Take the left side and position it over the wire at the front of the lamp.

3. And it produces a tiny loop on the left side of the lamp wire under the right side of the thread.

4. Then take the proper string and position it behind the wire of the lamp.

5. Via the tiny loop that you formed on the left side of the lamp wire, pull the whole length of it.

6. Repeat it out, your tiny heart. The design will continue to swirl as you make more and more knots. The spiral will travel in the same

direction as long as you start from the left side and take it over the top of the lamp wire. If you take over the right hand or bring the wrong side under the spiral, the instructions will turn, and the knots will have to be undone.

7.   It is time to wire a socket until all of our knots are finished. If you like, you can do this until you start knotting. It's all up to you.

8.   You'll want some cup or planter for your socket protection. We will use a thrifted copper cup for our lights and a sale plastic cup from Target to paint it white with spray. You should use something, though. A wooden tub, a ceramic planter, the sky's the limit too.

9.   Start by drilling into the bottom of your cup a hole.

10.   And mount the threaded nipple to the socket base (make sure you tighten the tiny screw on the side such that when you twist the light bulb, the plug does not unscrew.)

11.   Place the washer, then the cup, then the base of the plug over the lamp's wire. Connect the socket according to the given instructions.

12.   And screw the washer onto the threaded nipple.

13.   Slide the rope up and around the end of the threaded nipple (this is the only change you won't have to do if you wire the socket before beginning on your knots)—in-place the glue.

9. HEXAGON MACRAMÉ MUG COASTERS

Coasters are among your fast and simple projects. Thanks to all of our art projects, we have many types of coasters inside our house, and we don't use them most of the time.

Those are all super basic hexagon coasters that need just 2 macramé knots: the double-half hitch knot and the square knot.

The way we're going to make square knots is a bit different than normal. You will tie a standard square knot with each, but you will attach one-half knot to that. But rather than a square knot, it is a half square knot.

This way, joining the square knots tends to render each knot look "square," making the hexagon form look correct. At first, we attempted this with regular square ties, and it turned out to feel all squished.

We enjoy these macramé cup coasters with our coffee in the morning. They're good and wide and have tons of surface space for the large size coffee mugs.

It does not take long for this project to be made, and you might batch a couple of them at once with your dowel to save time.

Materials

- 3-millimeter single strand

- 12 pieces (64 inches tall) macramé cord

- 1 piece long (35 inches) macramé cord

- Sharp scissors

- Stiffening mist

- Fringe brush

- Wooden dowel

Instructions

1. Tie the cords to both the dowel with both the lark's head knots. With lark's head knots, tie the 12 (64 inches) large pieces of string to your dowel. It does not matter how big the dowel is at the top, and we're going to take it off the dowel. We just want it to be ready to hang on our shelf.

2. Tie a string of double-half a hitch ties. Take the first 6 of the cords and that the last 6 of the cords and tie them out from the reach and above the dowel. Pick the 35 inches long bit of rope immediately. You're supposed to use that as a filling cord for a series of 12 double-half hitch knots around the end. It may be a little difficult to have the first double-half hitch knot. However, the rest is much simpler when you get it aligned.

3. Switch the edges of the filling rope above the dowel just out of the path, and then the half-square knots are ready to be tied. Tie a standard square knot beginning with the 4 cords on the left side. And bind an extra half of the square knot to complete the knot. That is how all your square knots will be, and it certainly keeps them "square" a bit more.

4. In the first row, you'll attach 3, then pull down 2 cords on the left side and 2 cords on the right side. Tie 4 for the next line, moving from the first line. For the next 2 lines, repeat that method, inserting an additional knot for each line.

5. If you have reached the 4th line with 6 knots, you can decrease with one knot the next line, ignoring 2 extra cords at the start and end of each row before hitting the last row of 3 knots.

6. Taking the coaster to a worktop and slip this off the dowel so all the major knots are attached. We have to slice the looped cords from the coaster's both ends before attaching the double-half hitch knots. We just do not have to slice the highest ones yet (above the double-half hitch knots row that we did already). Anyway, we'll come to it.

7. Keep wrapping knots over the double-half hitch. Protect macramé board from the coaster. For each corner, put a needle to it to keep in position as you operate. We can see that the filling cord's direction would take to the boundary of a double-half-hitch knot. In the bottom left section, the 2 edges of the filler chord pass over.

8.   Tie a line of the double-half hitch knots for any fringe cord across, beginning at the lower corner. Switch the board a little as you hit a corner and continue moving towards the next corner. We will turn it over and tied the opposite hand so the 2 edges of the filler string are touched. We will repeat it on the 2 sides to the right. Then knot the filling cords with one final double-half hitch knot using the left cord here as filler to close it off.

9.   Sliced off the big portion of the fringe. Trim off the majority of fringe. We cut it down to 1 1/2 inches or so. Even with your preferred fringe brush, brush it out nicely. At this phase, if you like, apply any stiffening spray, and afterward, brush that out again until it dries. Cut it down once more, cut that to about 1/2 inches in length this time. You are done.

10. DIY MACRAMÉ RAINBOW

Really this macramé rainbow is pretty fun to create, and without awful hand cramps, you might whip up many of them in one day.

Materials

- Macramé cotton cord 25 mm. single strand cut to the below lengths: 14 inches, 11 inches, and 9 inches

- 4 yarn colors you like (mix different types and thicknesses of yarn freely. We used wool, cotton, and acrylic that we had laying around)

- A thick felt piece that is approximate. 6.5x8.5 inches

- 7 inches string piece for the hanger (we used macramé cotton string 3 mm. single strand, but jute, twine, or anything you've on hand you can use)

- Tape for the cord ends

- Sharp Scissors

- Hot glue gun and glue sticks

- Fringe brush

Instructions

1. You have to trim down the filler cords to the required size. We have the lengths we used mentioned above in the list.

2. Until you cut it, make sure the rope is wrapped with tape around the spots you're about to cut because this material unravels and frays like mad. We just wrap it and then cut the tape piece right in the center.

3. For the rainbow yarn options, now it is time for the rainbow bands to wrap up. For this one, we're using some random yarn from my stash, and they are all different kinds of yarn.

4. For wrapping the bands, begin by keeping down the yarn end where you're going to wrap it. On the filler cord right side, then begin wrapping tightly, concealing the end.

5. Continue to wrap all the way left, leaving on either end the same quantity of uncovered filler cord.

6. Trim the yarn and thread it into a broad eye needle until you've had

it all wrapped. Then feed the needle and yarn down through 2/3 wraps and tie a knot for securing.

7. The yarn end is then fed down through many wraps, and the yarn flush with the wraps is trimmed.

8. Now you have the first rainbow band done.

9. For the remaining bands, repeat these steps. Line them with the previous band until the ends are tied off and check that the yarn finishes and begins at the same spot.

10. Before tying it up, you may have to strip or add some wraps.

11. evening the rainbow bands.

12. This is time to glue them until you have all the bands wrapped.

13. Before you really glue the parts down, we suggest having a test fit. This way, you sort of know where it's all going to go. They're trapped when you hot glue them.

14. We are starting with the tiniest band. Add the hot glue to the back of the wrapped part of the yarn. Then rapidly push it down into position and keep it for a sec to cool the glue.

15. In the middle, add the hanger until you begin to glue the other bands. Please be sure to line this so that the rainbow does not hang crooked.

16. Then simply go one at a while to glue the rainbow bands before they are all glued together. Push them together tightly because there are no holes between the bands.

17. It's time to trim it as everything is glued on.

18. We cut the filler cords' long ends first, and the tape is removed.

19. Flip it over and gently cut the extra felt down. Be cautious not to unintentionally cut the yarn/hanger, and neatly trim the felt so that you cannot see from the front.

20. Brush off the fringe and give it a trim after the felt is trimmed fully. Done.

Chapter 9
Personal Projects

11. MACRAMÉ BRAIDED FRIENDSHIP BRACELET

Materials

- 1 arms-length black wax cotton cord (5 mm.)

- 1 arms-length tan wax cotton cord (5 mm.)

- 1 arms-length natural (cream) wax cotton cord (5 mm.)

- Jeweler's glue or clear nail enamel

Instructions

1.   First, cut 3 strands of cord about 1 arms-length wide. Wax cotton cord holds up pretty much to everyday wear and tear. I braided with black, tan, and cream-colored cords.

2.   Fold the black cord in half, and crease the top to mark the midway point of the bracelet. Unfold the cord. About 4 inches down from the crease, pinch one end of the cord in each hand. Twist the cord really tightly until it starts to buckle, and fold the twisted part in half. You ought to have about 2 inches of cutely twisted cord.

3.   Take the other 2 cords, and fold them in half also. Line them up at the bottom of the twisted black cord, and tie a knot. Pull the knot tight.

4.   Separate the cords, the 2 light-colored ones are on the surface and the dark-colored ones are on the in. You ought to have 6 cords total, but we can braid them as 4 cords by grouping the light-colored cords. The alternating width of the cords looks interesting when it's finished.

5.   It's time to braid! Braiding with 4 cords is like braiding with 3.

6.   Bring the outermost cord on the left across to the center-right side. Then bring the outermost cord on the right across to the center-left side. Keep the braid flat and check that the light-colored strands do not twist around each other when braided into a single strand. Alternating colors look better this way.

7.   Continue in this pattern until the bracelet is long enough to suit your wrist.

8.   Finish the top the same way you began the braid. Pinch the top of the finished braid. You can seal it with a clip. Take one of the black cords,

and crease it in half about 6 inches down. Unfold the cord. Pinch either end 4 inches down. Twist the top opposite the braid until the cord begins to buckle. Fold the cord in half, and it should twist into a cute line.

9. Unclip the braid, gather all of the cords, and tie a knot at the bottom of the braid. The twisted black cord should backtrack and are available out the braided end.

10. Clip the stray cords off both ends of the bracelet, and seal with jeweler's glue or clear nail enamel.

11. Now, you can finish with the clasp. Tie a knot at the ends of the twisted black cord. Use a lighter strand of cord for the clasp—I used the clippings from the bracelet. Line the 2 twisted black cords up as you are going to wear the bracelet.

12. Cross the lighter cord over and under the black cords, the ends are protruding from either side.

13. Make a little loop in the right-side cord, and cross it under. Take the left cord under the top of the right cord (which is now on the left side) and send it through the loop you only made on the right side. Pull tight.

14. Next, do the same thing on the left side. Make a little loop in the left side cord, and cross it under. Take the right cord under the top of the left cord (which is now on the right side) and send it through the loop you only made on the left side. Pull tight.

15. Since a clasp is pretty small, we can finish it after just these 2 loops. Loosely make 3 more of those loops. Don't pull the cord tight.

16. Turn the bracelet over, and send the ends of the cord through the back of the loops you only made. Now you will tighten the loops to seal

the cord in place.

17. Carefully tighten each loop by pulling on the surface loop, working your way to the top.

18. Then pull the ends of the cords to tighten the clasp. Don't pull too tight—the bracelet must be able to slide on and off. Clip the cord and seal with the jeweler's glue or clear nail enamel.

19. That's it! You ought to have a gorgeous macramé friendship bracelet for fall with a sliding clasp!

12. MACRAMÉ BOTTLE VASES

Materials

- Clean and dry bottles, labels removed

- 4 pieces (1.25 m. each) jute or twine; and a little more to make the handle and base

- Scissors

Instructions

1. Start with an arm's length of twine. Loop around the neck of the bottle and weave the ends around to make a sturdy base.

2. Fold 1 of the 1.25 m. long pieces of twine in half, and insert the center point behind the bottom. Pull the ends through the loop and tighten.

3. Repeat until you have at least 4 evenly spaced pairs.

4. The right-hand side should loop under and over on the first knot, then over and under on the 2nd knot. This makes a square knot that will lay flat and keep its tension.

5. Repeat the knot on the other side.

6. Keep alternating pairs as you go along. Pull the work right down to see the planning as you are used. Experiment with spacing to get a net you prefer.

7. Secure the macramé to the bottom of the bottle with a few square knots. Make sure the twine is tied tightly and won't easily ignore.

8. Knot the ends using a knot, this point with no space between knots. Tie off and trim the ends.

9. Use a few +60 cm. lengths of twine to add handles. Loop over the bottom on the other sides of the bottle. Tie the handles together at the top and hang as desired! It is perfect for a floral display in the garden.

13. DIY MACRAMÉ PLANT HOLDER

Materials

- Metal or wooden ring
- Yarn
- Scissors

- Potted plant

Instructions

1. Cut 4 equal lengths of yarn. Mine were about 2 feet long—you want to make sure you have enough to finish your macramé plant holder! Depending on how large your planter is, you will need to make your yarn strands even longer.

2. Fold your yarn strands in half, then loop the folded end through your ring. Take the loose ends and pull them through the loop of yarn you have created and pull taut.

3. Separate the yarn into 4 groupings of 2 strands of yarn each.

4. Measure out several inches (I just eyeballed it), then tie each of the groupings together. Make sure the knots are all roughly the same length.

5. Take the left strand from each grouping and tie it to the right strand of the grouping next to it. Tie the knots a little above, only 1–2 inches from the first set of knots. I do know it sounds confusing, but I promise it is not! Take the 2 outermost strands and tie them together, forming a kind of a circular net.

6. Tie another round of knots, repeating the method of knotting the left strand of every grouping to the right strand of subsequent. Make the knots pretty close to the last round you probably did—only a 1/2–2 inches away.

7. Tie all the yarn strands in a knot a little bit below the last round of knots you made—about 1 inch. Cut off the excess yarn to make a reasonable tassel!

8. That's it! Just slip your planter into the macramé plant holder for a dangling beauty that will bring style to anywhere you set it!

14. MACRAMÉ SQUARE COASTERS

Materials

- Scissors

- Baby cotton yarn

- Measuring tape

- Paper tape

- Comb

- Yarn needle

- Rubber band

- 20 cords (100 cm.)

- 2 cardboard sticks (3 cm. width)

Instructions

1. First, make a loop near the top of a 150 cm. cord.

2. Then, fold one of the 75 cm. cords in half and place it under the loop of the 150 cm. cord, then make a cow hitch knot by bringing the ends to the opening we just created. Repeat this step 3 more times.

3. Next, pull the top of the 150 cm. cord to tighten the loop.

4. Use an elastic band to mark the first string you are getting to wave to keep track of every round.

5. Then, bring your holding cord to the right of the first string, make number 4 with the first string over the holding cord, and pull the top through the loop created. Repeat this another time to make a double-half hitch knot.

6. Repeat the same steps for the subsequent string then forth until you finish the first round.

7. Continue repeating these steps until you have got achieved 11 rounds.

Notes: When starting new rounds, you will notice some gaps between the last string and the first string. To repair this, you will add more cords to fill in space. The cord lengths don't need to be precise, so if you are 1 inch short it is totally fine.

15. JAR HANGER

This macramé project is very easy; you can make it in only 5 minutes! It is an ideal way to practice your first knots! Macramé is one of those things that seems really complicated until you sit down and check it out, then you realize it is not that tough.

Materials

- Scissors

- Jars (In case you skipped ahead, I used Yoplait Oui yogurt jars)

- Macramé Cording—I used this macramé cording and it worked great

Instructions

1. Measure your cording. You can make this as long or short as you want.

2. Length of hanger x 2 + length of jar + 10 inches—I chose 18 inches for my hanger length, so I measured that out with the cord twice, then added on the peak of my jar, then added another 10 inches and cut my cord there.

3. Now that you have your first piece of cording cut, you need to chop 3 more pieces of the same length. For a complete of 4 equal pieces of cording.

4. Fold the cords in half. Tie a knot at the top of the fold. This is the lovable little hanger part. Pack up the knot by tugging on the cords so that it is nice and neat.

5. Now hang it in front of something—a cupboard knob, a doorknob, etc. I found it much easier to tie the knots when it had been.

6. Take any 2 cords and tie a knot a little way down. Make the knots even all the way around.

7. Now, take 2 of the knots you only made and grab 1 cord from all of these knots and tie those cords alongside another knot. Go all the way around until you have 4 knots. Make sure they are all equal. This is your 2nd row of knots and you will see the hanger start forming.

8. Repeat step 6 and make another 3rd row of knots. With these little jars, I found 3 rows of knots to be the best.

9. Put your little jar in there and make sure it fits. If it doesn't, then just adjust your knots a little or stretch them out as much as you can. If it does slot in there, then just tie all the loose ends at the bottom into an enormous knot. This big knot is going to be the bottom of your jar hanger.

10. You will trim the excess hanging from the knot or keep it long. Stuff each jar with the fairy lights. Now hang them up and enjoy.

16. HANGING

You have probably seen those giant extravagant macramé wall hangings. Well, everyone has got to start somewhere! So here may be a simple yet stylish version for a beginner!

Macramé is IN, so now's the time to bust out your knot-tying skills. With all the displays at Urban Outfitters and macramé curtains lighting up, we had to form our rendition of this wall art trend. Instead of creating a standard macramé project with rope, we used an alternate material: jersey fabric! It worked magically. The top result was a stunning hanging that might be perfect to hold in your house, use as a backdrop at a celebration, or maybe as chic DIY wedding decor. Plus, you need 2 materials to form it!

Materials

- Jersey fabric

- Fabric scissors

Instructions

1. Cut thin strips of cloth approximately 1 inch by 10 feet. (Knotting the material makes the final project much shorter. Our 10-foot strips created a 3 ½ foot wall hanging).

2. Fold a cloth strip in half and slide the loop end under the dowel. String the open ends of the material through the loop and pull it tight to secure it over the dowel. Repeat with each strip of cloth, placing them about 1 inch apart until you reach the top of the dowel.

3. Make a row of basic knots, tightening them as close to the dowel as you want (we left about 1 inch between our knot and dowel).

4. Make a row of knots a couple of inches below your initial row of basic knots (read above for step-by-step square knot instructions!). Then, right underneath, add a 2nd row of square knots using the same fabric strips, creating a double-square knot pattern.

5. Move a couple of inches below, and add another row of square knots starting 2 strips in from the edge. Then, right underneath, add a 3rd row of square knots using the same fabric strips, creating the same double-square knot pattern.

6. Move a couple of inches below, and make another row of square knots using the material strips from the first row. Then, right underneath, add a 4th row of square knots using the same fabric strips, creating the

same double-square knot pattern.

7. Catch on? Create additional rows of knots (either double-square or basic knots) until your design is complete.

8. Cut the ends of the material strips so that they are even. Your shortest strip will determine the length of your hanging.

17. MACRAMÉ WATCH BAND

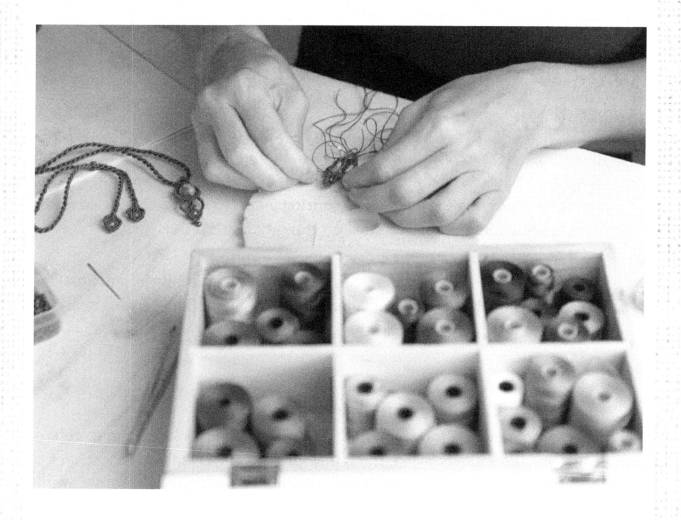

Give a thoughtful and fun gift to your bestie by making matching ally watches with crocheted bands! This friendship bracelet watch goes after the braiding trend with gusto and style!

Materials

- 1 watch face with posts

- Craft floss or embroidery floss

- Crimp ends (optional)

- Jump rings and closure (optional)

Instructions

1. To get started, you will need your watch face and your floss. I'm. using craft floss in orange, white, and a minty blue sort of color. Cut strips that are about 48 inches long. For this watch face, you will need 10 of those long strands for every side (but only cut 10 immediately, leave the others until you are able to start on the other side).

2. We're getting to lash each bit of floss onto the bar to start making our strap. Put the top side of 1 long piece of floss together and grab the end. Push it through the bar, then pull the ends through the loop.

3. Pull tight to latch on.

4. Continue this for all of your cuts of floss. Make sure to take care of the colors as you would like them in your pattern. I wanted thick stripes of orange and mint and thinner strips of white. As a result, my order went: orange, orange, white, mint, mint, mint, mint, white, orange, orange.

5. And now you only start your friendship braiding. Because we latched onto the post, we're not getting to have that weird bunched up thing that happens on most friendship bracelets that begin with a knot. Pretty cool, huh?

6. You have the choice of braiding the ends like all other friendship bracelets, then tying them closed once you wear them. This isn't the prettiest option, but it'll work rather well. But if you would like to use closures, you can do it.

7. When you get the length you would like to, take a good amount of glue and run a line where you will need to cut. Rub the glue into the threads on both the front and back sides. This may keep the braid firmly together for our next step. I used Aleene's quick dry tacky glue because I'm. horribly impatient.

8. After a couple of wears, I've had to shorten my straps. You will want to go ahead and make the watch a weensy bit tight. It's going to be uncomfortable that first wear, but it'll be perfect a couple of hours in.

9. Use sharp scissors to chop through your strap in the area you applied the glue. Plow ahead and run a little on the very end to assist prevent fraying.

10. Place your clamp onto the top of the straps and use pliers to clamp tightly on.

11. Finish the ends with a jump ring on one and a jump ring and closure on the other.

12. And there you have got it! It's a reasonably fun watch to wear and brings in the whole friendship bracelet trend in a new way. What does one think? Will you be making one up? seems like an excellent weekend project to me!

18. MACRAMÉ YARN GARLAND

Now, this is often a very great beginner project, so you can get used to tying those knots and still be proud of your final project. The best thing about this project is how it adds a lot of color and interest without having plenty of time or materials, which makes it an ideal project for table backdrops at parties or a marriage.

Materials

- Chunky yarn in similar thicknesses in a sort of colors

- Scissors

- Washi tape or push pins

Instructions

1. Cut one length of yarn for your base as long as you'd like. I cut mine to be about 8 feet long. Then hack lengths of yarn that are between 2-3 feet long depending on what proportion fringe you would like to hold down. You can always trim these up to be even later, but as you knot them together, they'll get shorter. I spaced my yarn out every 2 inches, then spread them out even more after I tied my knots. You will only need about 30-35 individual cuts of yarn to suit this size garland.

2. I hung my base strand to the wall with push pins then added my individual pieces by tying one knot over the bottom.

3. Then I started my 2nd row of knots by skipping the first strand of yarn and tying a double knot with the 2nd and 3rd strands. I centered it about 2 inches down from the bottom.

4. Then I continued tying the subsequent 2 strands of yarn together about 2 inches down, ensuring they were mostly centered between the knots on the bottom piece of yarn.

5. Then I started my 2nd row of knots where I started but tied a knot with the first strand and the 2nd strand. Then I continued to tie knots all the way across about 2 inches below the last knot. Once I used to be through with my 2nd row, I went back to the left side. I left my first strand alone and knotted the 2nd and 3rd strands again and repeated the method all the way across.

6. You can cut off here or keep going with more rows of knots, but I wanted a little fringe left. Your last step is trimming your ends to form them even and you are done!

19. MACRAMÉ STONE NECKLACES

Boast to your friends about your trendy macramé stone necklace and tell them how you made it and if they need one too!

I love nature, and I especially love it once I can incorporate it into my accessories. It's going to be stone or wood beads, a floral motif, or in today's case: pieces of actual nature because the hero of this DIY necklace is a stone.

I chose to use bright embroidery floss for this DIY stone necklace project, but any cord to fit your style will work! If you prefer a more subtle color scheme, then hemp, jute, or cotton cord in any color also will work well to capture objects like stones.

Materials

- Brightly-colored embroidery floss

- River rock(s)

- 4 mm. chain, 24–36 inches per necklace, depending on your preference

- 6 mm. split rings

- Lobster clasp

- Large eye needle

- Scissors

- Pliers (you may find split ring pliers especially helpful)

Instructions

1. First, cut 4 cords to a length of roughly 18 inches. This was plenty to hide a 2-3 inches stone. If your stone is smaller, you won't need the maximum amount length, but it's always better to have much than not enough!

2. Take 1 cord and string on a split ring. (You can substitute a daily jump ring, but this ensures that it won't take off your chain later.) Position the ring in the center of the string, and tie it around the other 3 cords at their center point. This may create a central ring with 8 (9 inches) strands knotted together at the center.

3. Next, pair up 2 cords that are next to every other. Tie a knot in both of them, connecting them, about 1/2 inch from the center ring in each pair of cords.

4. Separate the pairs of cords, and repair them with the neighboring cords. Tie another knot in each pair of cords about 1/2 inch from the first set of knots. You can still separate and alternate the pairs, creating knots a brief distance from the last set of knots.

Note: If your stone is particularly small, you may want to put the knots closer to the central ring and closer to every other. You are creating a kind of "net" to carry your stone, and the distance between knots will determine how large the holes are. Smaller stones will require smaller holes. You will have to experiment with your stones to find out the distances that are best for you.

- Try slipping your stone inside the internet as you are used, to work out if your sleeve may be a good fit.

- When you have created a large enough net to carry your stone, slip it inside and tie it tightly around the stone. Here's a tip to get it tight—separate the cords into 2 parts, and tie them together in the way you'd tie a shoe. Double-knot it to get it very tight around the stone. Then, tie a knot around the double knot (which you can also call a square knot) to end it for appearance.

- Trim off the ends to make a tassel, and your DIY stone necklace pendant is complete!

- Optionally, you can brighten up your chain to match your stone pendant by performing some simple weaving. Cut a length of embroidery floss that's 6–8 inches longer than your chain. Tie a knot at one end of the chain, and string the floss onto a large eye needle. Weave the floss back and forth through the chain, tying a knot to the opposite end of the chain to secure it.

- String your pendant. Then connect a hoop to at least one end of your chain and a hoop and lobster clasp to the opposite end to end your DIY stone necklace. Don't forget that you can adapt it to any item that's difficult to drill to string differently.

20. MACRAMÉ LAPTOP MAT

Protect your laptop from stains and rough table surfaces while giving your desk table a macramé uplift. This laptop mat also provides comfort for your wrist while you type away throughout your busy workday.

Materials

- Wooden board
- 4–5 clips
- Scissors

- Measuring tape

- Size

- 25 cm. (9.8 feet) x 45 cm. (17.7 feet) yarn

Instructions

1. Measure and cut 48 pieces of 3 m. (9.8 feet) yarn. Leaving approximately 10 cm. (3.9 inches) yarn, secure the yarns to a wooden board using 4–5 clips to start knotting.

2. Continue:

   - 1st row: Tie 12 square knots from left to right.

   - 2nd row: Skip the first 2 strands. Create a knot with 2 strands from the first knot and a couple of strands from the 2nd knot of the first row. Continue knotting 10 more square knots to possess 11 square knots in a row.

   - 3rd to 10th row: Make rows of square knots, skipping the first 2 strands for the 4th, 6th, 8th, and 10th row.

   - 11th row: Complete a row of horizontal double knots.

   - 12th row: Skip 3 strands and knot subsequent 5 square knots.

   - 13th row: Skip 5 strands and knot subsequent 4 square knots.

   - 14th row: Skip 7 strands and knot subsequent 3 square knots.

   - 15th row: Skip 9 strands and knot subsequent 2 square knots.

- 16th row: Skip 11 strands and knot subsequent 1 knot.

- Return to 12th row: Using the 3rd strand of the holding cord, tie 10 double knots from left to right diagonally down. Using the 24th strand of the holding cord, tie 10 double knots from right to left diagonally down. Skip the 25th strand and knot subsequent 5 square knots.

- Return to 13th row: Skip the 25th to 27th strand and knot subsequent 4 square knots.

- Return to 14th row: Skip the 25th to 29th strand and knot subsequent 3 square knots.

- Return to 15th row: Skip the 25th to 31st strand and knot subsequent 2 square knots.

- Return to 16th row: Skip the 25th to 33rd strand and knot subsequent 1 square knot.

- Return to 12th row: Using the 25th strand of the holding cord, tie 10 double knots from left to right diagonally down. Using the 46th strand of the holding cord, tie 10 double knots from right to left diagonally down.

- 13th to 21st row: Tie square knots to make a diamond pattern.

- Continue knotting the pattern with square knots and diagonal double knots until you get the pattern.

- 33rd row: Complete a row of horizontal double knots.

- 34th to 43rd row: Make rows of square knots, skipping the first 2 strands for the 34th, 36th, 38th, 40th, 42nd rows.

3. End: Cut off both ends neat and even to lengths of your preference.

21. MACRAMÉ DREAMER

To call this a dream catcher doesn't do it justice. This stunning hanging would look great in a nursery, bedroom, or anywhere in your home.

Materials

- 40 mm. ring
- 175 mm. ring
- 420 mm. ring
- Twine

Instructions

1. Using a 40 mm. ring, I larks head knot the twine onto the ring, then

create the spiral know work using a half knot twist.

2. I spiral out all the way until I'm. able to add a subsequent 175 mm. ring.

3. More twine is then larks headed all the way around on the 175 mm. ring (making it appear as if a really attractive sea creature), at now there's a lot of twine to wrangle!

4. The final 420 mm. ring is attached and now some serious macramé knots can happen.

22. MACRAMÉ TABLE RUNNER

Macramé is such a rewarding craft technique. Once you have got a couple of simple knots under your belt, you can create endless combinations to form lovely, one-of-a-kind pieces for your home. This DIY macramé table runner only uses one sort of knot over and over to make a gorgeous woven pattern that brings a boho vibe to your tabletop. It is the perfect project to tackle with friends or while you are watching your favorite movie. The table runner comes together quickly and your guests will certainly be asking where you purchased it!

Materials

- Scissors
- Macramé cord
- Masking tape

Instructions

1. Cut your cords. Start by cutting your macramé cord into 12 pieces, each 15 feet long. It helps to wrap each end of every cord with masking paper to avoid fraying as you are working with the cords. Arrange cords on the ground or at a table where you are comfortable working, spreading them to make sure they are not tangled or knotted.

2. Knot in pairs. Next, knot the cords into pairs of 2. You ought to find yourself with 6 pairs of cords, each knotted. Make sure to go away with about 10 inches of cord hanging free on the top of the knots. This may be one end of your table runner.

3. Start a knot. Now you can start creating the knots, which will weave together to make your table runner. First, separate the 4 leftmost strands of the cord. Push the others aside to offer yourself some space to work. Bring the left cord over the top of the opposite 3 cords, creating the form of a loose number "4."

4. Continue the knot. Now, bring the right cord over the top of the left cord that you just moved. Bring the tail of the right cord under the center 2 cords, then upward through the center of your "4," and up to the left.

5. Pull ends. Gently pull the 2 outer cords together so that the knot starts to make. Leave about 2 inches from the bottom of your original

knots to permit for spacing. Now you have completed the first half of your first knot.

6.   Finish the first knot. Now you will repeat the method of steps 3-5, but mirrored and starting with the rightmost cord. Start by taking the right cord (from your group of 4 cords) and laying it over the remaining 3 cords. Then place the left cord over the top of the right cord you only moved.

7.   Pull taut. Bring that left cord under the 2 center cords, then up through and over the right cord. Pull the 2 side cords taut to satisfy the other half of your knot. Now you have got completed the first knot.

8.   Create another knot. Make another knot, repeating steps 3-7, right underneath your first knot

9.   Move to the subsequent section. Now that you know the knots you will be creating, keep going! Advance to subsequent 4 cords. Repeat the method of tying 2 square knots using these 4 cords. At this point, you will want to start out being conscious of the space between knots and the way much excess cord you allow therein space. Do your best to form it evenly throughout your table runner as you are used your way along. This may create the most even, polished final product possible. Once you finish 2 square knots with the center 4 cords, advance to the rightmost 4 cords and make 2 square knots there also.

10.   Create another row. You have completed your first row! To move on to the subsequent row, start by setting aside the 2 cords on the left and the 2 cords on the right. You will be dealing only with the center 8 cords for this row. Create 2 square knots with the 4 left cords first. Then create 2 square knots with the 4 right cords. This may complete your 2nd row.

11.   Continue the knotting process. For the 3rd row, bring all of the cords back together and make 3 double square knots even as you probably did

for the first row (in steps 3-9). Then create your 4th row by repeating step 10. Continue this process of alternating rows of 3 and 2 until your table runner is long enough for your table!

12.   As you create knots, do your best to stay your knots equally taut and spaced.

13.   Finishing the table runner. Once your runner is long enough for your table, finish it in the same way you started it. Create pairs of 2 cords each, and knot them together. Then trim the ends to 10 inches of excess cord past the knots to match the opposite end. Remove the masking paper from the opposite end of the runner.

14.   Place on your table. Put that lovely runner on your table! After you lay it down, you will find that it needs a little adjustment here or there to stretch or space the sections out.

15.   Add your home settings and the other table decor you wish. Enjoy!

23. PLANT HANGER WITH CERAMIC BOWLS

Making one macramé plant holder is pretty straightforward, but making one with multiple levels may be a little more complicated.

This project is sort of simple to make, very affordable, and can turn any corner into an attention-grabbing decor.

Materials

- 3 ceramic bowls
- 30 yards of rope
- Ruler
- 1 curtain wooden ring
- Scissors
- Super glue
- Some nice plants

Instructions

1. You will start by making the rope support to carry each bowl. Cut 8 pieces of rope of 30 inches each.

2. Make a knot at one end to carry the 8 pieces together. Don't hesitate to tighten!

3. Take a bowl and place it upside down, put the knot on the center, and separate the 8 strings 2 by 2 to form a cross shape. Make a knot, at 2–3 inches from the center, to carry every pair of the string together.

4. Take one string from each pair and join them with a knot, the rope between the first and the 2nd row of knots will form a diamond shape.

5. Once you finish making the 4 knots of the 2nd row, repeat the same process to make the 3rd row of 4 knots.

6.   If you use regular bowl size, 3 rows of knots are going to be enough to carry them. The rope holder must be large enough to carry the bowl completely into it.

7.   Repeat the previous steps to make the rope support for every bowl. I made a 3 level planter, but it'll work as find with more bowls if you have got room for it!

8.   Now you would like to connect all of your bowl supports together to make your hanging planter. Cut 2 pieces of rope of 3 yards. Fold them in the center and make a loop with them, passing the rope through the wooden ring. You want to have 4 strings of 1 1/2 yard hanging from the ring.

9.   Attach each string with a knot to the first rope support. Try to have the same distance between the ring and every knot you create, help yourself using the ruler, and make a little mark on each rope at a distance of 25 inches from the ring. It's important if you would like your bowl planters to carry horizontally!

10.   Then attach the 2nd and the 3rd rope support below the first one, leaving an area of roughly 12 inches between each. Cut the additional rope length of every knot if necessary and add a dot of superglue. As the planter can become a little heavy when watering, this may stop the knots from slipping.

11.   Put your plants into the bowls. You can add some pebbles in the bottom before putting the soil and your plant as there's no drain hole.

12.   The last item you would like to do is drilling a hole in the ceiling and screw a hook. Use the wooden ring to hold your rope planter first, then place your bowls' planters into each rope support.

13.   Enjoy your new green decor!

24. MACRAMÉ UMBRELLA TASSELS

Materials

- Outdoor umbrella—honestly, any kind of color are going to be perfect
- Macramé cotton cord
- Scissors
- Sewing needle
- Sewing thread—the similar or same color of the umbrella

Instructions

The steps below are getting to show you details on the way to make the perimeter for one section of your umbrella. Depending on how many sections/ribs you have on your umbrella, you will need to repeat everything times that.

1. Cut a bit of macramé cord. As a first step, cut a bit of macramé string that's a little longer than ONE section of your umbrella. Then secure the road to both ends of the umbrella ribs.

2. Cut 18 pieces of macramé strings. Measure and cut 18 (4 feet long) macramé strings and fasten them onto the string you already secured onto your umbrella.

3. Macramé square knots. Attach the macramé strings using square knots. Repeat this step for 3 rows.

4. Cut off the excess macramé. Cut off the excess macramé pieces. Then untangle your twisted fringes. If you are not using a twisted cord, you won't have anything to untangle.

25. MACRAMÉ BLANKET

Before we start, I assumed I'd allow you to know that this particular tutorial is for a little, newborn-sized blanket and takes approximately 1 hour to finish. I assumed this is the simplest size to start with, especially if you don't have any prior experience. Every blanket size requires a special amount of yarn, and it takes 4 pounds to form the baby blanket in this tutorial.

Materials

- Super chunky merino wool
- Your own 2 hands
- A clean surface (I usually use the floor!)

Instructions

1. Begin by unraveling an honest amount of your merino wool. That way, you have got enough wool to work with without having to tug at it, which may cause it to interrupt.

2. First, you want to sew. To do this, you create a loop at the top of your wool. You are doing this by placing your working yarn over the top of the yarn. Place your hand inside the loop, grab the working yarn, and pull it through. You have essentially just made an error knot in the yarn. This is often your first official stitch.

3. To make the 2nd stitch, put your hand through the first stitch and pull the working yarn through it. Make an identical-sized stitch as your first for consistency. To make a looser chunky knit blanket, make sure not to make your stitch loops too small. To make a baby blanket, make approximately 20 stitches across in your first row.

Tip: To count your stitches if you lose track, just count the number of holes you have in the row that you are hand knitting.

4.   Now that you have created a sequence of 20 stitches, it's time to start the 2nd row of your blanket. Take the last stitch, put your hand inside the loop, and grab the working yarn and pull it through. Repeat this process by moving left down the chain of stitch holes until you come to the last one again. Put your hand through each loop, pull your working yarn through, and repeat for 20 stitches.

5.   Repeat number 4, except that you will knit to the right side in this stitch and alternate every subsequent row. Continue knitting until you run out of yarn.

6.   Now let's find out how to remove (it's super easy, a bit like the rest of the blanket!). To remove, take 2 stitches with the working yarn behind them, put your hand inside the 2 stitches, grab your working yarn and pull it through. You now have 1 stitch made up of 2 stitches. Repeat this step by picking up a 2nd stitch and pulling the working yarn, as long as you knit 1 stitch from 2. Repeat this until you reach the end of the row.

7.   Create your last stitch and use the top of the yarn to tie a knot, completing your blanket. You can either tuck the excess yarn back to the blanket to cover it or cut off any extra length. Yay! You did it!

8.   You should now have your very first completed chunky hand-knitted blanket.

26. HANGING MACRAMÉ GARDEN

Why not make your little garden using these mini macramé plant hangers?

This idea is super cute and adds interest to the spices and herbs you have got growing in your garden.

Materials

- I needed a sturdier pole than a wooden dowel, so I opted for a skinny metal dowel, 48 inches long. Now to start the weaving.

- Rope

Instructions

1. Cut 32 pieces of rope, each measuring approximately 120 inches. Tie them onto the pole, using a lark's head knot. I used 5/16 inches wide nylon rope for this hanging because it will withstand the weather better than cotton. It took nearly 4 rolls of 100 feet nylon rope.

2. Group the cords into 4 sections of 16 (individual cords). Using the knot, weave a "V" shape into each section.

3. Repeat the 2nd row of "V" shaped knot knots for all 4 sections. Then tie a knot at the bottom center of every of the 4 Vs.

4. In the 3 spaces between the Vs, tie another knot 3 in total.

5. Beginning with the 16 individual cords on the far right side, about 4 inches down from the center V knot, make a row of 3 square knots. Let the 2 individual cords on each end hang loose.

6. Now about 2.5 inches beneath that row, make the 2nd row of 4 alternating square knots.

7. About 2.5 inches down from the 2nd row, make the 3rd row of 3 alternating square knots.

8. To create the "pocket" for a flower pot or mason jar, using the 2 loose cords on each end of the last row, make the 4th knot. Bring the 2 cords from each end around to the front; using those 4 cords, make the knot. This creates a circular shape to the present section of the hanging.

9. Now you are able to finish the pocket with a wrapped knot. About 3

inches down from the last row of square knots, tie a wrapped knot. Then cut the rope ends to your required length.

10. Now you have got created a pocket for your first flower pot, using the 16 cords on the far right of your hanging (the 4th section). Repeat steps 5 through 8 for the 16 cords on the left of your hanging (1st section).

11. For the 2nd set of 16 cords, follow steps 5 through 8. Now about 2.5 inches down from the 3rd row of square knots (which has taken on a circular shape), make another row of alternating square knots. Then, about 2 inches down, tie a wrapped knot. You now have 3 sections done!

12. You should have pockets for 3 flower pots done (sections 1, 2, and 4). For the remaining 3rd section of 16 cords, follow steps 5 through 7. Then make the 4th row of 4 alternating square knots. Again, make the 5th row of 3 alternating square knots, and using the 2 loose cords on the ends, make another knot in the front to make a circular pity pocket (see step 8).

13. Not quite done! Now make a 6th and final row of 3 alternating square knots. Then make a wrapped knot to end it off.

14. Your hanging should now have 4 completed sections with pockets for flower pots or mason jars. You can cut the tassels to any desired length. I prefer a staggered effect.

15. I used small ceramic pots that measured 2.5 inches bottom diameter and 4.5 inches top diameter. Fill them with dirt and your favorite herbs, then place them in the pockets. If you don't want the upkeep of daily watering, use succulents planted in pretty containers instead. Better yet, even faux succulents would look beautiful (especially if you are displaying the hanging indoors.) This sweet macramé hanging garden was well worth the work.

27. MACRAMÉ ROOM DIVIDER

This macramé room divider lends itself easily to creating a bohemian and relaxed atmosphere while defining an area. Not only does it let in plenty of light, but it is another surface to place some plants—Perfect for the studio, shared office space, or gigantic room in need of definition. All it takes is that the right of rope, a couple of simple knots, and the kind of patience these big projects sometimes require. Spoiler alert: It's always worthwhile.

Materials

- 1 (36 inches) wooden dowel

- 3 (700 feet of 1/4 inches) strand cotton rope

- 3 (3 inches) hook screws

- Scissors

- Air plants (optional)

Instructions

1. For this specific project, you will want to live out 24 strands that measure 28 feet long each. This may offer you a hanging that measures roughly 7 feet from the top dowel to the bottom dowel and you will add length to it with fringe on the bottom. If you are eager to design a shorter piece, it's always better to still use more rope than you think you will need.

2. Now are 2 finished lark's head knots, then the beginning of a 3rd. You will need 2 strands of rope per knot for a complete of 12 knots. Fold 2 strands in half and place the center of this pair of rope strands over the top of your first wooden dowel. Then wrap them around your dowel and pull the loose ends down through your loop. You have probably done this knot before and not even known it. No pun intended.

3. Continue adding your pairs of rope strands to the dowel until you are finished. Be mindful that you are wrapping over the top of the dowel consistently. If you forget and wrap one under the dowel instead, it'll change the design of your pattern. Make sure all of your finished lark's head knots are spaced equally aside from one another.

4. We'll use a half knot further down in the design to feature subtle contrast, but it also makes up the first step of the knot, so I'm. showing it first. A half knot requires 4 strands of rope. The 2 center ropes stay where they are and the 2 outer ropes shy away just a bit. Then create a bend in the outer left rope and move it towards then under the outer right rope.

5. Then bend the outer right rope under the place where the outer left rope crossed it, behind the 2 center ropes, and copy through the bend from the outer left rope.

6. We can use this knot on its own in a bit, but this is often also the first half of the knot you can use for the first section of the divider.

7. This is comprised of 2 half knots. Repeat the same pattern you probably did in the step above, on the other hand, pull the outer 2 rope strands until that last half knot rests snugly against the first half knot. Now you have made a square knot! Repeat this process on each of your pairs of rope strands for your first row of knots.

8. You will have 12 square knots in your first row. To make your 2nd row of square knots, you will be using 2 strands from one knot and 2 strands from the knot next to it to make a new knot that joins them together. You can start from the center of your piece and work your solution on either side (how I prefer to do it) or you can start from one side and move your way across. As you can see, once you get to the sides of your 2nd row, you will have an additional pair of rope strands on all sides. That's next.

9. When you are adding in your knots, be mindful of the space between each row. You don't want to start out tying things closer and closer together or you will find yourself with a lopsided hanging. Sometimes it is helpful to step back about 6 feet to look at your composition before continuing. Trust me, you won't want to later realize it is crooked enough to be annoying.

10. For this design, I'm. allowing about 2.5 inches of space between all of my knots because I would like the space divider to feel light and airy. Once I add in my 3rd row of knots, I'll be back to my original pattern using all of the strands. The space that your outer rope creates on absolutely the left side of your divider then the right side of your divider should be a little bit longer than twice as long as that. You would like it to possess

enough slack to make a scallop shape. My scallops held their shape in some parts of my divider but got heavy in other parts. I'm. assuming it's tricky to get that good but do your best.

11. For my pattern, I did 4 alternating rows of square knots, then switched it up and did 6 alternating rows of half knots. Then I finished up the rest of the divider with 13 alternating rows of square knots again. These kept things feeling consistent enough to form a press release but also added a little of a subtle design change to stay it from looking like I'd hung a hammock from the ceiling!

12. To add the bottom dowel to your room divider, you are getting to create more lark's head knots. You can't create them the same way you started, so we're doing it backward. I've started with a couple of already attached to point out you ways it'll look when it's done.

13. Separate the 4 strands underneath one of your square knots and set 2 aside.

14. Wrap the opposite 2 strands all the way around the dowel until you wrap inside and over the top of the same 2 strands.

15. Wrap them on the opposite side of the strands and back behind the dowel.

16. Continue around the front of the dowel and tuck under the loop you only made. It'll leave a fringe down the backside of the dowel. This is often only one of the 2 lark's head knots you will make per knot.

17. Bring the opposite 2 strands from that knot back over and wrap them around the dowel and to the left side.

18. Wrap them over the top of themselves.

19.   Wrap them behind the shank and every one of them behind and under the loop you just created.

20.   Scoot that knot in close to the first one you made and make sure things are consistently taut. Repeat with each of the opposite strands in each knot.

21.   Trim your fringe to the length you would like. We have 10-foot ceilings, so albeit this room divider is very large, I had to hold it from the screws in my ceiling with another 18 inches of rope.

28. DIY HANGING MACRAMÉ CHAIR

Materials

- The materials used for the project were from the house Depot and that I used over 8 packages of this rope. I think I used 8–9 (200 feet) packages plus 1 (100 feet) package—That quantity, including the rope that I used to hang the chair, which is braided also. This is often a large chair and it used a lot of rope.

- Hula hoop

Instructions

1. The most important thing I might say is to make sure you have got enough rope which the rope is long enough. I began by cutting 60 (10 feet) pieces of rope, that wasn't enough. I lost count after a short time, but I think I ended up using around 120 (10 feet) pieces of rope for just the walls of the chair. But before you only cut away, use plain tape and put it around the rope and cut on the tape, that way you don't have the rope unravel.

2. I started with doing a basic knot around the hoop. I then did alternate square knots around the whole chair. I started on the left and that I worked my way around.

3. At this point, I used to be feeling very excited and hopeful that I used to be getting to be ready to pull this chair off. After quite a few hours, I began to meet up with to the seat a part of the chair and this is often where my first little bit of trial and error happened. This failed because I just kept making my way right down to the seat using that very same knot. So, I had to require that apart.

4. After brooding about it for a short time, I found out I needed a 2nd hoop, but I also needed it to be a little lighter. So, I used a smaller hula hoop and after I sprayed that white, I placed it where the seat would go and to make sure it might fit.

5. After I made sure the ring would fit, I then took it out and did the seat as a completely separate piece. So as to do the seat, I used a bit of poster board and I pinned a bit of rope to it.

6. The only reason I did this was that I wanted to be ready to make just a straight piece about the dimensions of the seat to be ready to then tie it onto the loop. The poster board helped.

7.   I just used this rope on the poster board to assist hold the form I wanted to do the seat. I still did the alternating knot. I tied the seat knots a little more spaced out because I wanted to possess a special look on the seat.

8.   After I finished the seat I tied the walls of the chair by tying a basic knot around the little hula hoop and then tied another basic knot to tie the seat to the hula hoop as well.

9.   Once the seat and walls were tied to the hula hoop, I tied the tails of the walls and the tails of the seat very carefully so I could have a little more support.

10.   The tails had to be cut off. A bit like the hen I cut the rope for the chair I had to glue each piece together before cutting.

11.   I made an easy braid for the ropes that support the chair and using some pieces of wood I had around the house I cut 4 pieces of the same length and drilled holes where the rope would go. The hardest part was leveling and tying the wood evenly.

12.   This chair can be a lot of work. But I will be able to say that it's not that hard and it's usually nice. It just takes time. I hope you learn from my mistakes.

29. MACRAMÉ PLAY TENT

Materials

- 2 twin flat sheets
- Hula hoop

- Steel craft ring

- 22 sets of bronze grommets

- Grommet tool

- Hot glue gun

- Hot glue sticks

- 2 spools of macramé rope

- 1-2 spools of cotton crafting twine (depending on what percentage of tassels you make)

- Scissors

- Needle and thread or home appliance (optional)

Instructions

1. To start making my boho macramé play tent, I started by hot gluing the macramé rope all the way around the hula hoop. This not only strengthened the hula hoop because they are apparently made from paper now (?!?!?), but it also hid the ugly purple and sparkle stripes. Not that there's anything wrong with purple and sparkles but, for this project, I actually didn't want to see it.

2. To make sure the string is securely in place, I add a bead of hot glue 1-2 inches long and then quickly wrap the string around the hoop by pushing it into the glue.

3. Next, I cut 10 strands of the macramé rope (110 inches each) and 10 strands of the cotton twine (110 inches each).

4. Mistake #1: I know this looks like a lot of rope but trust me, you will need it, and if you don't do that the first time like me, you will end up very frustrated and annoyed once you need to untie everything and begin over.

5. I attached the rope to the ring by folding the rope in half and looping it over the ring, then pulling the ends of the rope back through the loop.

6. After hanging my steel loop on a hook so that I could clearly see all of the rope, I began to tie my knots. To do this, I first worked with the macramé rope and ignored the cotton string. I started by taking a piece of string from each strand and tying it to the nearest neighboring strand with an easy knot. To finish the circle, I tied one strand from each of the top sections to each of the opposing pieces. This is usually a must for making a rope circle. You'll also want all the knots to be as close together as possible when you look through the rope. My first row of knots was approximately 3 inches from the steel ring.

7. To make the next row of knots I completed the same steps approximately 3 inches from the first row of knots, except at this point I tied each section of rope next to its original partner. Again tying the 2 end pieces together behind the planning. This can give the rope the diamond pattern back and forth when opened.

8. Mistake #2: Each row of knots should increase the distance between them at every joint or every other joint, depending on how long or short you want the top area of the macramé to be. If you tie them all the same distance apart every time. Your design is going to be more intricate but, you will also end up with a very long macramé top area that doesn't open up enough to allow the hula hoop to fit. Leaving you once again frustrated and with sore fingers once you need to untie everything and start over. To

avoid this fit the pattern I finally ended up using it like this:

- Row 1: 3 inches from steel ring

- Row 2: 3 inches from the previous row

- Row 3: 3.5 inches from the previous row

- Row 4: 4 inches from the previous row

- Row 5: 5 inches from the previous row

- Row 6: 6 inches from the previous row

9. Once all the macramé rope was tied, I opened up the planning and tied it around the perimeter of the hula hoop, taking the time to evenly space each section. Next, it was time to tie the cotton string. I used the same process for this layer, except I tied each knot at the same distance between the 2 macramé knots. This way, the planning would stay on top of the twined design without impeding the previous layer. It is vital to remember to fasten the 2 end sections double around the back of the rope layer.

10. Once all my cotton twine was knotted, I tied it to the hula hoop and spent a couple of minutes deciding where the back of my tent would be. This way, once the sheets are added, the hoop will hang level, as the back is going to support a little more weight than the front to allow for the opening.

11. To add the draped panels, I first hemmed the hem that would normally be at the top of the bed and sewed. Creating a small layer of fabric that was 4 levels thick. Although this step is optional, I find that the buttonholes hold better on thicker fabrics or multiple layers of fabric.

12. I then measured and marked every 6.5 inches starting with a mark about 1 inch from the edge of each sheet. Then, using my scissors, I cut a small hole through the layers at each mark. Next, using my grommet tool I applied a grommet to each hole—with a total of 11 grommets per sheet.

13. Once this process was completed on the 2 flat sheets I added tied my sheet to my hoop over the overlap of the last 2 grommets on each sheet on the backside. This overlap will help prevent gaps when hanging the tent.

14. To create my tassels, I wrapped the white cotton cord around the back of my dining chair 15 times. For the macramé cord tassels, 6 times. Next, I gently slid the string, tied it in the center with a short length of twine, and wrapped it around the top of the tassel with the opposite string/cord because of the tassel, and secured it with hot glue. Once it was securely tied, I cut all the loops off the bottom and used the scissors to even out the jagged edges and get a nice finish.

15. When it came time to attach the tassels to the tent, I removed the small piece of twine from the top and ran the twine section of the tent. This helped cut down most of the twine. I attached a tassel to each of the eyelets to complete 10 tassels, 5 cotton twine, and 5 macramé cords.

16. Now my boho macramé play tent was finally done and prepared to be hung! I will be able to say the results are beautiful! Who would know I haven't been macraméing since 1970? Well, except maybe for the very fact that I wasn't alive in 1970!

30. MACRAMÉ PLACEMAT

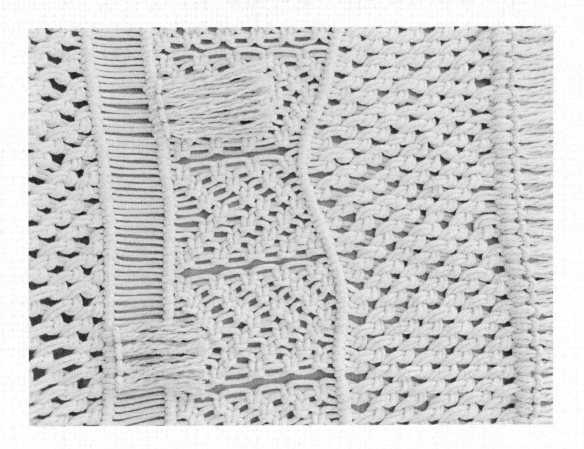

Macramé placemats are an ideal addition to your table.

Materials

- Cording
- Sharp scissors
- Hanger

Instructions

1. Start by cutting 20 pieces of cords, each 116 inches long. This part

is tedious, I know.

2. Attach each of the 20 cords to your hanger using lark's head knots.

3. Leave an area of about 1.5 inches and from there make a row of square knots, followed by a row of alternating square knots.

4. Continue this pattern until you have got 5 rows of square knots.

5. Take 8 adjacent cords, and tie a knot with the 2 cords in the center. Each of those "center" cords are going to be used as your leader cord. One center cord is going to be worked on the diagonal to the left and the other to the right. We are making a diamond shape. Woot!

6. Take the center cord on the right and place it over the 3 cords to the right. Attach each of the 3 cords using double-half hitch knots. Take the center cord on the left and place it over the 3 cords to the left. Attach each of those 3 cords using double-half hitch knots. You ought to have a triangle shape once you are finished! Do you see it?

7. Now—take your leader cords and push them aside for a moment. You are going to make a knot in the center of the triangle. Rather than having 2 center cords, you will have 4!

8. Continue making the bottom of the diamond shape by creating double-half hitch knots but working it towards the center.

9. Once your 2 rows of double-half hitch knots meet in the center, just tie a little knot. This helps tighten it together.

10. Now, we are back to creating 5 rows of square knots!

11. Repeat the same pattern 3 times (5 rows of square knots, diamond

with double knot and knot in center).

12. Once you are finished with your pattern, cut your placemat off the hanger, slightly below the lark's head knots.

13. Hang your placemat evenly over your hanger or fold it in half. Trim the opposite side of the placemat so that it's even with the first side you narrow off.

31. MACRAMÉ MASON JARS

This macramé project is ideal for you because: It uses regular mason jars and it uses basic macramé knots—nothing complicated here, folks.

Materials

- Macramé cord
- Scissors
- Mason jars

Instructions

1. Let's start by cutting the cords we'd like.

2. For this project, I made 2 jars. 1 regular-sized Mason jar and 1 larger-sized Mason jar with a handle.

3. I cut the cords all the same lengths for both jars—you will need to cut off some excess on the regular-sized jar at the top. But it's always better to possess an excessive amount of cord than too little!

4. For each jar, your cord will be 6 feet long each.

5. You will need 6 cords for the larger jar and 8 cords for the regular jar.

6. The patterns for every jar vary slightly:

7. The larger Mason jar with handle (known as Larger in this tutorial):

The pattern is one alternating knot all the way around. For the regular Mason jar (known as Regular in this tutorial): The pattern is 2 square knots followed by sets of 2 alternating square knots all the way around.

8. To begin each:

- Regular: Take 2 of your 6 feet cords and wrap them around the lip of the jar—secure them with a knot.

- Larger: Take one of your 6 feet cords and wrap them around the lip of the jar—secure with a daily knot.

9. Attach the rest of your cords:

- Regular: Take the rest of your 6 cords and fasten them to your jar using reverse lark's head knots.

- Larger: Take the rest of your 5 cords and fasten them to your jar using reverse lark's head knots. Evenly space the knots all around the lip of the jar.

10. Tie square knots:

- Regular: Make 2 square knots all the way around.

- Larger: Make a row of 1 alternating knot all the way around the jar.

11. Continue the pattern down:

- Regular: Now make a row of 2 alternating square knots. Continue these rows of alternating square knots until you get to the bottom of the jar.

- Larger: Continue with another row of alternating square knots all the way around. Do that until you reach the bottom of the jar.

12. Hint: Do you have a handle on your jar? Just work around it by making your knots around or through the handle.

13. Finish: Regular/Larger: Once you get to the bottom of the jar, cut off some excess rope but leave a little there and comb them out for a fringe look.

32. MACRAMÉ ROPE AND DOWEL PLANTER

It's time for an additional monthly DIY challenge!

Materials

- Rope
- Dowel rod
- Glue gun

Instructions

1. I began by staining my dowel rod in my attend stain color—dark walnut. Then I coated it with some poly to seal it up.

2. Next, you will want to chop a very long piece of rope and begin wrapping it around one end of your dowel about 1 inch approximately from the top. Use your hot glue gun to attach down both ends, then measure what proportion rope you would like at the top for hanging, then still wrap the rest of the rope around the opposite end of your dowel.

3. Now you can totally leave it like this and use some "s" hooks or other sorts of hooks to hold a plant or anything from, but I took it a little further.

33. MACRAMÉ SPIRAL BRACELET

This fun macramé bracelet is straightforward enough for beginners to finish. This spiral knot pattern is popular for friendship bracelets made with embroidery floss, but you can make this bracelet using any sort of macramé cord.

Materials

- Waxed cotton cord
- Scissors
- Clipboard

- Binder clips

- Washable fabric glue

- Charms

- Measuring tape

- Tapestry needle (optional)

- Self-adherent cling tape or band-aids to guard your skin

Instructions

1. Start by cutting your waxed cotton cord to a length of 220 cm./87 inches and 50 cm./20 inches. Tie the longest cord around your 2 shorter cords at about 8 cm./3 inches. In this manner, you will find yourself with 4 cords hanging from the starting knot. Arrange the 2 shorter cords in the center and the 2 longer cords on the surface. The shorter cords are going to be called anchor cords and the longer cords are going to be called tying cords.

2. The way to tie a half-knot which will naturally become a spiral. Pass the right tying cord over both anchor cords. Pass the left tying cord over the top of the right tying cord. Now pass the left tying cord under the anchor cords and through the loop formed by the right tying cord. Pull on both tying cords to tighten the knot. You have now completed your first half-knot! Repeat these steps to make a row of knots. After only a few knots you will see that your work will spiral naturally.

Tip: You will need to make a few knots and you will need to pull on tight. I began to get blisters on my finger really soon and used some self-adhesive cling tape to guard my fingers.

3.   Adding a charm to your macramé spiral bracelet. Continue tying knots until you have reached the length where you'd wish to add your charm (I did after 8 cm. / 3 inches of spiral knots). Slip the charm over the right tying cord and perform yet one more half-knot. Keep on knotting happily away until you have accomplished another 8 cm. / 3 inches or whatever length you would like.

4.   The way to finish up. Lay your bracelet around your wrist. If you are proud of the length of your bracelet, it's time to end things up. Make a daily knot. By using a darning needle as a little helper, you can easily guide or slide the knot to the very end of your knotted macramé spiral. You will need to insert it into the knot before you pull tight.

5.   How to make an adjustable sliding knot clasp using the macramé knot? Here are 5 simple steps:

• Cut a little over 30 cm./12 inches of your cord.

• Wrap your work around your fingers and keep the ends parallel to each other. Place the cord inside the center of your bracelet and tie the first knot in the center of the parallel ends of your work. Tip: If you don't pull as hard as you do for the bracelet knots, the sliding clasp will be easier to work with.

• Repeat making square knots. The amount will depend upon how wide you would like your adjustable sliding knot clasp to be. I'd say about 2–4 square knots.

• Cut the ends of the cord you have wont to tie the square knots closely to your work and dab them with washable fabric glue. Your adjustable sliding knot is complete.

• To finish things up, you can tie the 2 anchor cords together using a knot and trim the ends.

34. OPENWORK MACRAMÉ BRACELET

A lot of macramé projects look heavy—made with thick yarns and dense knotting patterns. Macramé also can be wont to create light and lacy looks, like in this bracelet. This openwork macramé style is delicate, pretty, and faster to knot than a denser pattern would be.

Materials

- 10 crochets cotton

- Clasp

- Jump rings

- Large rings—about 1/2 inch or 12–14 mm.

- Sharp scissors

- Sewing pins

- Cork panels

- Jewelry pliers

- Fray check or clear fabric glue

Instructions

1. Decide how long you'd like your bracelet to be (in inches or centimeters). Multiply your finished length by 11, then add 12 inches or 30 cm. to the number. Cut 8 strands this length.

2. Pin one of the massive rings down for resistance. Fold a strand in half, and make a lark's head knot.

3. Do that 3 more times (for now).

4. Bring the strand at the furthest left across the rest, and tie a double-half hitch knot around it with the strand next to it.

5. Tie double-half hitches with the remaining strands.

6. Bring the left side strand across again, and tie another row of double-half hitch knots.

7.   Do that another time and you ought to have 3 rows.

8.   Now repeat the same thing on the right, but opposite. Bring the farthest right strand across.

9.   Again, tie 3 rows of double-half hitch knots.

10.   At the top of the 3rd row, tie round the right-side strand with the strand closest to the center on the left. This may join the 2 sides of the work.

11.   On the left-hand side, starting the 2 strands closest to the center, tie a double knot. Use the strand on the left to tie round the strand on the right. This is at a 90° angle to the rows already worked.

12.   The strands will trade places.

13.   Do the same thing with the 2 strands to the left of what you only tied, then with each pair until you reach the edge.

14.   You should have 4 knots.

15.   Now bring that farthest left strand across and tie double-half hitches such as you did in the first 3 rows. Make sure to keep the strands. Placing a pin at the corner will help keep the work even.

16.   When that row is tied, do 2 more rows as before.

17.   On the right side, tie a double knot with the 2 strands closest to the center.

18.   Do the same with the remaining 3 pairs.

19. Place a pin at the corner, and do 3 full rows of double knots.

20. At the top of the 3rd row, tie around the center-right strand with the center-left strand to hitch the edges.

21. Repeat this motif—one row of paired double-half hitches, 3 rows of ordinary, and joining at the center—until you are one large ring in need of your required length.

22. Do a row of the paired half hitches.

23. Bring the left side strand across and tie it around it. Don't let it rejoin the opposite strands.

24. Bring subsequent strand across and tie around it with about the first strand. Don't let it rejoin the opposite strands.

25. Tie around each strand until you are right down to one strand doing the tying.

26. The left side is completed for now.

27. Repeat the same thing on the right—a row of paired double-half hitches, then bring the right-side strand across and knot around it.

28. Tie around each strand without letting it rejoin the opposite strands until you are right down to one strand on this side.

29. Now it's time to feature the ring.

30. Flip the work vertically. Slide the 2 left-most strands through the ring. Bring the strands around.

31. Tie a knot with the 2 strands, ensuring the ring is tight to the rows of double

32. knots.

33. Bring subsequent strand through

34. Then bring the 4th strand through the ring. Tie a knot with this pair of strands.

35. Keep repeating that with each pair of strands until all are tied.

36. Tie a row of double-half hitches on the left. Try to pull the strands toward the

37. center so that they don't hang over the edge and show on the front.

38. Let the strand from the left join the strands on the right. Tie a row of double-half hitches on the right side.

39. Do another left and another right-side row.

40. Apply a coat of fray check or clear fabric glue to the 2 rows of knots and let it dry completely. Then trim the additional crochet thread very carefully.

41. Add a clasp and it's able to wear!

35. MACRAMÉ RAINBOW ORNAMENTS

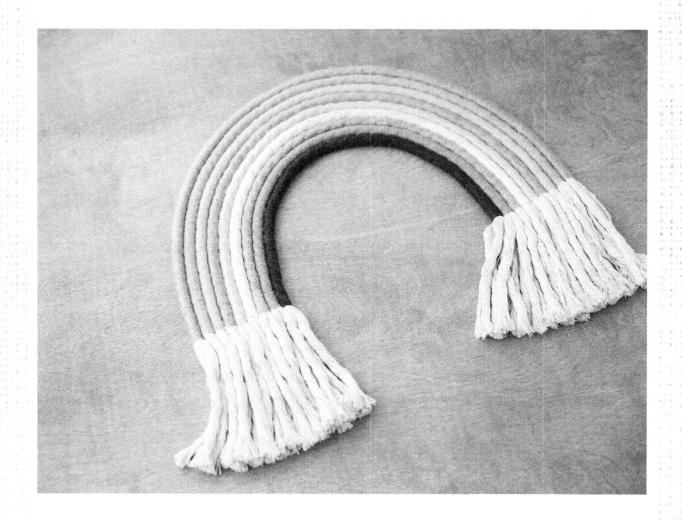

Materials

- 3 colors of yarn
- Wooden beads (14 mm.)
- Stainless steel wire
- Rope

- Glue

- Scissors

Instructions

1. Shape rope into 3 arch shapes.

2. Make your rainbow keychains.

3. Cut rope ends off, make sure to go away the frayed yarn for the rainbow "clouds."

4. Measure wire to individual rope and move size.

5. Tie the yarn to the top of the rainbow (making sure the wire and string are inside) and wrap it up to cover the wire and string, and tie it off at the other end.

6. When all 3 rainbow bows are covered with string, tie a piece of string to the top rainbow.

7. Glue the 3 rainbow bows together. (You can also sew, but I find it easier to glue.)

8. Add wooden beads to the dangling piece of yarn, tie a knot with the yarn to make a loop, and attach it to the tree or enlarge a stocking.

36. GIANT AGATE MACRAMÉ JEWELRY PENDANT

Materials

- Macramé yarn

- Sharp scissors

- Agate slice of your preferred color

- Hot glue gun

- Packaging tape or adhesive tape

- Yarn needle

Instructions

1. Measure the circumference of the agate slice: I wanted a very large blue slice of agate to match all my blue shibori pillows. Agate slices are so pretty with all their variations. I chose the blue tear-drop-shaped one and used my leftover macramé yarn. If you use a smaller slice, then you have got to use thinner macramé yarn. Mine is 4 mm. yarn, so go right down to 1 mm., 2 mm., or 3 mm. yarn for smaller slices. You can make several of them and string them onto a garland, too which might look awesome.

2. Cut a bit of macramé yarn that's about 10–20 inches longer than the circumference of the agate slice and tape it to a solid surface on both ends to stay in place and have tight tension on the yarn.

3. I chose the space to be 2 inches, but you ought to pick something that applies to the dimensions of your stone. If it's smaller than 1 inch might do.

4. Loop lark's head knots on all sides of the taped-down string. Make sure that every one of these strings is about 4 times longer than the circumference of your agate slice.

5. Then loop vertical double-half hitch knots on all sides. I feel they ought to be called pretzel knots because that's precisely the shape you have got to duplicate over the taped-down string.

6. Then keep taking place the strings by crossover. Make sure to always have the same side of string cross over to form it look cleaner.

7. Keep going until you can fit the whole band of knotted strings around the slice. And make sure that you keep the width of the band (2 inches in my case) all the way to the top.

8. The next step is where you merely wrap the macramé band around the slice and knot.

9. Then you have got a tail left at the top of the wrapped stone that you need to tightly enclose with a replacement string of square knots.

10. The 2 center strings would be the bunch of strings from the stone wrapping.

11. Next, you have got to fold the knotted strings over to make a loop.

12. This is where you will need the glue gun. I cut the strings shorter and glued the ends so that they wouldn't fray, then tied and knotted the longest string around the loop.

13. Finally, you have to thread the ends through part of the macramé with a thread needle and then cut the ends so that they are completely hidden.

14. You can tie the wrapped macramé stone to a handbag with a jeans scrap. And that I thought that wrapping a little crafting mirror with macramé yarn would look great too and be useful one a handbag for once you need to refresh your makeup—or with a reasonably little scarf. Otherwise, I prefer tying tassels or items just like the wrapped stone to doorknobs or maybe curtain tie-backs.

15. I also love the piece of wrapped stone macramé jewelry strung onto a strand of huge wood beads. It's literally sort of a giant necklace for your home. If you would like to travel with this look and buy or make a garland, then make sure that the loop is long/large enough to suit the beads.

37. HOME ACCENT MACRAMÉ RUG

Materials

- 514 feet jute rope (¼ inch diameter) 28 (18 feet lengths) pieces and 2 (5 feet lengths) pieces

- Washi or masking paper

- Supported Dowel or Hanging Dowel

Instructions

1. Tape off a 22 inches workspace on the dowel.

2. Mount all 28 (18 feet) ropes on the dowel using lark's head knots and space them evenly across the workspace.

3. Ranging from the center of a lark's head knot, measure 7 inches around the dowel and down the front of the leftmost cord. Mark now with a bit of tape. Repeat on the right; then connect the 2 points by gently securing a length of tape horizontally across all of the cords, ensuring they continue to be evenly spaced and aren't twisted.

4. Knotting. Make sure to tighten each horizontal double knot only enough to stay positioned directly below the lark's head knot above it. If your knots aren't tight enough, then you will find this row wider than you'd like. If they are too tight, the row is going to be too narrow. Take care not to incorporate the ends of the filler cord into the next knotting.

5. Leaving an 8 inches tail, work a row of horizontal double knots from left to right around one of the 5 feet ropes using the tape line as a guide and removing it as you are used your way across.

6. Work 19 alternating rows of 2 square knots, or until you have roughly 12 inches of rope remaining on each cord. Make sure to finish with a row that has square knots at its left and right edges.

7. Directly below the last row of 2 square knots, work a row of horizontal double knots from left to right using the opposite 5 feet rope of the filler cord, and again leaving an approximately 8 inches-long tail in the filler cord before knotting.

8. Finishing. Trim all of the cords along the bottom edge, also as both ends of the filler cords from the 2 rows of horizontal double knot, to about 7 inches.

9. To make fringe at the top, cut each rope at the center of its lark's head knot. Snip one near the center first, then work your answer toward the sides.

38. WOOL AND YARN MACRAMÉ WREATH

Materials

- 2 inches opportunity

- 28 (22 inches length) strings macramé yarn

- 14 (8 inches) pieces thick wool

- Comb

- Scissors

- Fabric stiffener (optional)

Instructions

1. I began my wreath by folding the 22 inches pieces of macramé yarn in half and looping them onto the opportunity with lark's head knots

2. This will form a decent circle of yarn which will be sectioned into 7 groups of 8 strings.

3. Take the string on the surface of 1 of the grouped yarn strings and loop diagonal knot knots towards the center of the group.

4. Half hitch knots are basically loops placed on the outer string on all sides that then meet at the center of the group in a triangular shape.

5. Repeat the same concept of the knot knots another time around the circle.

6. You will find yourself with short ends, which I trimmed, then combed out the sides a little before beginning to weave the thick wool yarn into the piece.

7. You have to use the center of the triangular shapes to loop and weave the short pieces of wool through. Almost like a lark's head knot. Go all the way around the wreath.

8. In the end, you can spray the wool with a fabric stiffener to make sure that the wreath doesn't lose shape.

39. MACRAMÉ HANGING—HALF-CIRCLE (SEMI-LUNAR)

Materials

- 7 pieces of 94 inches 4 mm. natural cotton macramé rope (3-ply twisted or single strand will work, I used 3-ply)

- 6 pieces of 63 inches 3–4 mm. mustard cotton macramé string (or whatever color you prefer, this will be 3-ply twisted or single strand, I used 3 mm. single strand, but it might probably be better if all of the rope was the same diameter. It's what I had available, so I went with it.)

- Wooden dowel to carry your work

- Sharp scissors

Instructions

Row 1:

1. Attach 2 of the long ropes to the dowel with a lark's head knot.

2. Tie 2 ropes on with lark's head knots

3. Using the 2nd rope from the left as your filler rope (ignore the first rope), make 2 double-half hitch knots to the right.

4. Tie 2 double-half hitch knots to the right

5. Attach the filler rope to the dowel with a lark's head knot.

6. Attach it to the dowel with a lark's head knot

7. The first row of DIY macramé hanging completed

Row 2:

1. Attach another long rope to the dowel on the right side with a lark's head knot.

2. Attach subsequent pieces of rope on the right with a lark's head knot

3. Using the 2nd rope from the right as your filler rope, make 2 double-half hitch knots to the left.

4. Add a bit of mustard rope to your filler rope with a cow hitch (reverse lark's head) knot.

5. Add a bit of contrasting rope in the center.

6. Pull the knot nice and tight, then make 2 more double-half hitch knots across to the left.

7. Make 2 more double-half hitch knots to the left

8. Attach the filler rope to the dowel with a lark's head knot.

9. Attach the filler cord to the dowel with a lark's head knot

Row 3:

1. Add another long piece of rope with a lark's head knot to the left

side of the dowel.

2. Add the subsequent piece of rope on the left with a lark's head knot

3. Using the 2nd rope from the left as your filler cord, make 4 double-half hitch knots to the right.

4. Make 4 double-half hitch knots to the right.

5. Add another piece of mustard rope onto the filler cord with a cow hitch knot. Then make 4 more double-half hitch knots across to the right.

6. Add the additional contrasting piece to the center, then continue making 4 double-half hitch knots to the right.

7. Secure the filler cord to the dowel with a lark's head knot.

8. Attach filler cord to the dowel on the right with a lark's head knot

Row 4 and more:

1. Repeat these steps for every row. You can add additional pieces of mustard rope to the center in each row.

2. 7 rows finished on DIY macramé hanging

3. I cut off after 7 rows on this one, but I continued for 9 rows on the pink and blue versions.

4. DIY Macramé hanging with 3 colors: To get the 2-color effect, I added a bit of pink string to the center of rows 2–4 and a bit of blue string to the center of rows 5–8.

Finishing your DIY hanging:

1. Once you have done as many rows as you would like, you have got to make a decision on what you would like to do with the fringe.

2. For the mustard/natural one, I left the perimeter long and I decided it needed some more volume, so I tied another piece of string across the back and added more natural colored rope using a cow hitch knot.

Chapter 10
House Projects

40. PLANT HANGER

Macramé plant hanger is of the varied sorts of macramé which is regaining the eye it deserves. It involves tying knots to form beautiful ar2rks. If you are among those that find it difficult to form crafts or do not have the interest, the great news is: you have got an entire lot of already made ones to select from. Plant hangers are one of the most popular items in the beautiful art of macramé.

The counterculture generation had it right the first time. There's a health benefit in surrounding your family with flowers and green plants.

Materials

- Jute

- Scissors

- Something to hold your plant hanger

- Plants in small pots

Instructions

1. Start by making 9 pieces of jute twine to your required length. If you don't need the hanger to be extra-long and to accommodate a mean size plant, start with 100" pieces. Fold the strings in half, and tie a little string in the center. Once you hold the strings by that tiny string, you ought to find yourself with 18 pieces that are half the length you originally started with. Hang the project from a nail in the wall, so you can work with it more easily.

2. Divide the 18 strings into 3 sections with 6 strings each. Braid each section until you reach the specified length. For an extra-long plant

hanger, this may be approximately 24". For just a mean length, braid about 14". Tie a knot at the top of every braid. Next, go down from the braid knot about 6" (or less if you are making a small one). Divide the bottom of the braid in half so that you have 3 pieces on all sides. Join one braid to subsequent one over by tying 3 from each braid (6 totals) with a knot. Repeat in a circular fashion until all 3 braids are connected. Go down about another 6" (or less if you are making a small one) and make another row of knots.

3. Finish macramé plant hanger with a large knot. Finally, go down a final 6" and make one giant knot with all 18 pieces. Trim the strings. Place the potted plant into the macramé plant holder. That's it!

Well… it got me thinking how beautiful these plant hangers would be with tiny succulents. Just make the braid lengths and spaces between the knots smaller to permit such a little arrangement.

41. MACRAMÉ HANGING VASE

Macramé is enjoying its moment in the spotlight again after decades in craft exile. It is a really satisfying craft and the knots are easy to select up.

Materials

- 1 small round vase with a diameter of about 20 cm. (8 inches).

- 30 m. (33 yards) of 3 mm. (1/8 inch) thick nylon cord. Venetian blind cord is ideal. You can only use about 28 m., but it is best to have a bit more.

- Scissors

- Ruler or tape

- Masking tape

Instructions

1. Cut 8 cords measuring 3.2 m. (3.5 yards) each and put them to at least one side. Then cut one cord measuring 80 cm. (31.5 inches) and leave it. Finally, cut one cord measuring 1.4 m. (55 inches).

2. Set aside the 2 shorter lengths of cord. Group the 8 lengths and let the ends align. Fold them in half and mark the center with a bit of tape.

3. Hold the cords about 6 cm. down from the fold. Take the 80 cm. cord and hold it parallel to the most cords, with a tail of about 12 cm. below your grip. Make a loop out of the long section of the new cord and wrap the cord around the back of the most cord group. Keep your thumb on the short tail.

4. Continue wrapping the cord around the main cord group and over the loop, working your top. The wrap should be firm but not too tight. Make the loop bigger if you would like to. This adjustment will make the tail shorter.

5.   Wrap around 13 times, then thread the cord through the loop and pull down on the short tail (the one at the bottom of the wrap which you have been holding with your thumb) to shorten the loop.

6.   Continue to pull slowly on the short tail. The other end of the cord will get pulled into the wrap. If your wrap is just too tight, the cords won't pull through and you will need to start the wrap again and make it a bit looser. Cut off pulling when the 2 cords that overlap get to the center of the wrap. Cut both ends of the wrapped cord close to the wrap so that they cannot be seen.

7.   Divide the cords into 4 groups of 4 cords. Finish up and separately secure the ends of 3 of the groups with tape.

8.   Taking the unsecured group of cords, measure 29 cm. (11.5 inches) down from the wrap. Mark the measurement with a bit of tape and tie a knot (that's just a standard knot) under the tape. To make sure the knot finishes up in the correct place, tie it loosely, then slide it up into position before tightening it.

9.   Pick up the left-hand cord (cord 1) and fold it over the top of cords 2 and 3, then under the right-hand cord (cord 4).

10.   Then take cord 4 and fold it under cord 1 and behind cords 3 and 2, then up through the loop created by cord 1. Push it up so that it's right under the massive knot and pull both ends until the knot is firm. That's called a half-knot twist.

11.   Continue making half-knot twists the same way—always starting with the cord on your left. As you are doing this, the knots will form a twist and become a half-knot sinnet. Cut off once you have made 12 half-knot twists. Repeat with the remaining 3 groups of cords.

12.   Measure 9 cm. (3.5 inches) down each cord group and mark with

tape. Tie a knot under the tape.

13. Now we are getting to join 2 cord groups which are next to every other. Lay them side-by-side and filter 2 cords from each group. They are going to now form a replacement cord group.

14. It's been very easy thus far, hasn't it? So, now we come to the Josephine knots. They are a bit trickier but easy once you have done one.

15. To make sure your finished knot is flat, keep the cords flat as you tie them and do not allow them to overlap.

16. Start with the 2 cords on the left. Form a loop with the cords going behind. Bring the 2 right-hand cords over the top of the loop.

17. Loop the right-hand cords under the bottom-left cords and hold them in place with your left, then copy and over the top-left cords.

18. Next, thread the same cords behind the first loop and through the opening. Finally, thread them over the vertical left-hand cords and through the loop again.

19. While the knot is loose, place it in position: it will be 3 inches (7.5 cm.) below the knots in your hand. Flatten the cords so that they lie side by side and pull the 2 ends together until the knot is tight.

20. Continue dividing and joining each cord group to the subsequent one with Josephine knots. To make sure your macramé hanger hangs rightly when you are choosing which groups to hitch together, search at the wrap to see which of them are next to every other. For the 4th Josephine knot, you will be joining the 2 cords on the left with the 2 on the right.

21. Now we are getting to divide the cord groups once more. Measure 15 cm. (6 inches) down the new cord group and mark it with tape. We'll be tying 3 square knots, which are a variation on the twist knot.

22. For part one, begin the same way as the twist knot: pick up the left-hand cord (cord 1) and fold it over the top of cords 2 and 3, then under the right-hand cord (cord 4). Then take cord 4 and fold it under cord 1 and behind cords 3 and 2, then up through the loop created by cord 1. You have just done a half twist knot. The 2nd part is what forms the knot.

23. For part 2, now we are going to start with the right-hand cord. Pick up the right-hand cord (cord 4) and fold it over the top of cords 2 and 3, then under the left-hand cord (cord 1). Then take cord 1 and fold it under cord 1 and behind cords 3 and 2, then up through the loop created by cord 4. That completes the knot.

24. Repeat the entire knot (i.e., parts one and 2) 3 times. Then repeat on all 4 of the new cord groups.

25. This is where it becomes a bit fiddly because you will be bringing all the cords together at the bottom. Divide the cord groups one last time into 4 new groups of 4, remembering to group those that naturally hang next to every other. Laying your macramé flat on the table or hooking it over a door handle will help.

26. Tie one knot (refer to step 8) on each of the 4 new cord groups. All the cords will now close at the bottom.

27. Take the 1.4-meter cord and wrap the bottom of the hanger. Start the wrap about 6.5 cm. (2.5 inches) below the last square knots. The cord is wrapped around about 18 times or until it reaches and fits snugly against the last group of square knots. Follow the instructions in step 3 to form the wrap.

28.   Cut the cords to different random lengths and tie a knot close to the top of each one.

29.   Put water in your vase and arrange the flowers. I chose small blooms and cut the stems short so that they are contained in the vase. Longer stemmed flowers and leaves trailing over the edges would also look great. Hang the macramé hanger from a hook or an image rail. Then open up the space in the basket and place the vase inside.

30.   Cut off and smell the flowers.

Conclusion

This macramé art has become an essential part of international culture and tradition, employing macramé art that is used to create fashionable products. So far, widespread is the justification for macramé art for the world cultures majority and creates a tie connecting people of different cultural backgrounds. It must be remembered that through creativity and commercialization around cultures, it has experienced vast changes and expansion. Nevertheless, the macramé-designed product trend, primarily via cinemas, magazines, and the internet, has been noted to be driven by the extensive developments in apparel fashion. Macramé art, though, is also seen as a promising exportable opportunity that can be further grown to generate jobs and increase its contribution to the GDP (Gross Domestic Product). To further revitalize the global economy and culture, an initiative in this direction would go a long way.

Made in the USA
Columbia, SC
10 December 2021